The Life and Death of a Proud Azorean

The Life and Death of a Proud Azorean

A Biography

Roberto Machado

Roberto Machado

COPYRIGHT

Copyright © 2023 by Roberto A. Machado

All rights reserved. No part of this book may be reproduced in any manner whatsoever without written permission except in the case of brief quotations embodied in critical articles and reviews.

ISBN 978-1-7390220-3-7
Ebook ISBN 978-1-7390220-4-4

Printed in the United States of America

Published in Canada by Roberto Machado Presents

Cover design by Daniel Swanson
Photograph Insert design by Daniel Swanson

First Edition

DEDICATION

For my daughter, Natasha, who was fortunate enough to have the presence and love of her father until adulthood.

EPIGRAPH

¿Qué es la vida? Un frenesí.
¿Qué es la vida? Una ilusión,
una sombra, una ficción,
y el mayor bien es pequeño:
que toda la vida es sueño,
y los sueños sueños son.

La vida es sueño
Calderón

__ *Adieu, dit le renard. Voici mon secret. Il est très simple : on ne voit bien qu'avec le cœur. L'essentiel est invisible pour les yeux.*

Le Petit Prince
Saint-Exupéry

__ *Com efeito, não vale a pena fazer um esforço, correr com ânsia para coisa alguma.*
__ *Nem para o amor, nem para a glória, nem para o dinheiro, nem para o poder...*

Os Maias
Eça de Queirós

CONTENTS

COPYRIGHT iv
DEDICATION v
EPIGRAPH vi
PREFACE xi

ONE

Life Before the Tragedy

1 | In Ponta Delgada, São Miguel, Azores — 2

2 | Fate Rings the Doorbell — 4

3 | António's Youth — 8

4 | A Young Man Goes to Work — 12

5 | At Thirty, António Gets Married — 21

6 | Elzira's Early Years — 27

7 | Married Life in the Machado Household — 31

8 | Finally, a Son Is Born — 34

9 | António's Travel Adventures Outside of São Miguel — 41

CONTENTS

10 | Finding Business Partners in his Native Island 48

11 | António's Business Connections in the US 53

12 | Elzira's Sudden Ilness 57

13 | António's First Trip to Boston and New York 60

14 | A Brief Stopover in Bermuda Generates Two Postcards 63

15 | Four Letters and a Postcard Sent from the US 66

16 | Rekindling of an Old Flame 76

17 | The Secret Correspondence with Laura in 1960-61 81

TWO

The Tragedy

18 | The Fatal Second Trip to Boston and New York 104

19 | Awkwardly, António Asks Laura's Husband for a Favor 106

20 | An Idyllic Round Trip by Train from Boston to New York 109

CONTENTS

21 | Pleasure and Business in New York 113

22 | Unfinished Business in New York 118

23 | Two Postcards and a Letter Sent from Heaven 122

24 | In the Throes of Death 130

25 | A Woman in Distress 133

26 | Barely, Elzira Copes with Tragedy 139

27 | Chaotic Burial Arrangements 145

THREE

Life After the Tragedy

28 | Living with a Bully Again! 154

29 | Laura's Nineteen Letters to Elzira in 1961-62 158

30 | Virgínio Gets Mail from Laura Too 178

31 | A Business Loss 184

32 | The Challenging 1960s in Ponta Delgada 188

33 | Roberto's School Friends Save the Decade 193

CONTENTS

34 | In late 1975 Somerville, Massachusetts 201

35 | A Fresh Start for Elzira and Roberto in Toronto, Canada 205

EPILOGUE 211
ACKNOWLEDGMENTS 219
PHOTOGRAPH CREDITS 221
APPENDIX 223
ABOUT THE AUTHOR 251

PREFACE

The Life and Death of a Proud Azorean: A Biography has been a work-in-progress for decades. Its origins date back to the early 1980s when I discovered a treasure trove of documents carefully kept by my mother about my father's life and times. Upon reading it for the first time, in 1981, it triggered in the recesses of my brain a lot of mostly unpleasant memories from my late infancy and early adolescence during the 1950s and 1960s. I decided at the time that at some point in the future I would take a closer look at the material with the intent of threading a story based on it. In the meantime, the project was put on the backburner for future consideration as I was busy living my own life, especially establishing myself in my chosen profession: teaching languages at the high school level. The result? The years came and went and the story remained untold for lack of time until my retirement from the teaching profession in 2017. Finally, I had found the leisure to carry out this long overdue project. I was already in my mid-sixties. Irrespective of my age, the life-changing and unforgettable memories of 1961 came back to me as I took a deep dive into the documentation at my fingertips. Now, as I take stock of my own life, I realize that the factual events of 1961 conditioned the kind of man that I eventually became. So, getting this story off my chest and sharing it with you will be nothing short of cathartic.

My father's sudden demise at the age of forty-three turned the world upside down for my mother and me. António Augusto Machado was his name and he was a native of the island of São Miguel, in the Azores and, while on a business trip to the US, in 1961, he passed away unexpectedly in a hotel room of the Paramount Hotel, in New York, in the company of a woman who was not his wife. My mother's deep-rooted suspicion, as well as that of other family members and friends when this tragedy happened, was that he had been poisoned to death.

So, I will be relating, in the next chapters, the facts surrounding António's life and death based on the first-hand documentation, one that includes his numerous personal and business letters, official government dispatches addressed to him by his immediate hierarchical superiors, some of them by the Governador do Distrito Autónomo de Ponta Delgada (Governor of the Autonomous District of Ponta Delgada) himself praising the quality of his work and dedication, an official summary of his different government posts from 1939 to 1961 called Cadastro Geral dos Funcionários do Estado (Personal Dossier of the State's Civil Servants), postcards written to his wife and myself from a variety of places, including those mailed from Boston and New York in 1960 and 1961, a considerable number of photographs collected in neat family albums, newspaper clippings announcing his death, and even a six minutes long 8 mm film taken by one of his friends at the Joseph A. Costa Sons Memorial Funeral Home in Cambridge, Massachusetts, a suburb of Boston, where his wake took place.

In *The Life of a Proud Azorean: A Biography*, I put forth the views expressed by António's immediate family and friends surrounding the circumstances that led to the catastrophe to which, every now and then, I add my own opinions about the matter. As more and more details about his last days came to light, their initial suspicions became deep held convictions and those did not change with the passage of time in spite of the fact that nobody possessed the necessary concrete evidence to substantiate them. In other words, their firm beliefs were based on pure intuition and a basic understanding of human behavior.

Finally, the dialogues that appear in *The Life and Death of a Proud Azorean: A Biography* are a fabric of my own imagination and, as such, are a hybrid feature of this biography; my intention was to recreate the essence of the possible conversations that may, or may not, have taken place between the main protagonists at a given time and place while taking into consideration my knowledge of the personalities involved. Where quotes or italics are indicated, they are verbatim. Since most of them are in Portuguese, I have provided the English translation of the same.

ONE

Life Before the Tragedy

1

In Ponta Delgada, São Miguel, Azores

I woke up to a glorious summer morning on Tuesday, August 22nd, 1961, in Ponta Delgada, São Miguel, Azores. The sky was clear and there was a light breeze coming in from the Atlantic which meant that it would be a perfect day for kite flying, my favorite pastime during the long and lazy school holidays that were slowly but surely getting closer to an end.

That day, it was also my cousin's birthday and that meant that there would be a party in the evening attended by family and friends. It was going to be a perfect day, I thought, unaware that on the west side of the Atlantic, in New York, where my father had gone on a business trip, tragedy had struck in the early morning hours of that very same day, for he had died unexpectedly, changing the course of my life trajectory forever. For the time being, however, it was going to be a day of fun and games.

To record the eventful day for posterity, there is a black and white photograph, as most of them were developed in São Miguel in 1961, taken of four boys who are looking straight at the camera; it's about ten or, perhaps, eleven o'clock in the morning, a perfect time of the day for kite flying. They are all standing next to each other at the far end of the family house's backyard, and behind them is the vast blue Atlantic.

One of them, Carlos, is holding the spool with lots of string which is attached to a kite flying up high in the sky. He is turning six years old that day. Next to him stands a carefree and confident youngster who considers himself at the ripe age of nine an expert kite flyer. That's me, Roberto, his cousin, who had just turned nine years old myself on August 13th. As a birthday gift to my inexperienced cousin in matters related to kites, I am letting him hold the spool, something that does not require much expertise but that, nevertheless, does give one the pleasure of feeling the pull of the kite and the weight of the curved string leading to it. I am standing next to him just in case he lets go of the spool. One can never be too careful when flying kites.

Behind both of us, there are two neighborhood boys. They are my friends and they hang around with me most of the day every day, especially Eduardo Neves whose father died when he was very young. We are kindred spirits. So, we spend the carefree summer days going from adventure to adventure. There is nothing in the picture to suggest or foreshadow the terrible and devastating news that would disrupt Carlos' birthday party that evening, and that would change the course of two lives forever in particular: mine and my mother's. In the back of the photograph, one can read the following few words: *Ao querido Roberto do Carlinhos no dia dos seus anos*. (To dear Roberto from Charlie on his birthday.)

Many years have come and gone since that fateful August day, but every time that I look at that photograph and read the scarce words written on its back, I am reminded that life is marked by moments of happiness and pure joy intertwined with moments of sudden sadness and despair. One needs courage, fortitude, optimism and some moral support from a variety of people to deal with personal tragedy when it strikes, especially if one is young.

2

Fate Rings the Doorbell

The only event that struck me as extraordinary during my cousin's birthday party celebration that evening was that at one moment my uncle José, Carlos' father, and my own father's youngest brother, married to my mother's younger sister, turned off the music that was playing out loud and the party came abruptly to an end. No explanation for his unusual decision was given to the children in attendance and, as a result, all of us were left perplexed until someone said that the party was over and that we were to go to bed.

The reason, however, for the sudden end of the festivities was quite simple: A black car with four gentlemen inside who worked for the local government, the Governo Civil, had stopped in front of the family home and one of them had gotten out to ring the doorbell. When someone opened the door, the man asked to speak in confidence with José and showed him the telegram that had been received from the Consulate General of Portugal in New York which, in a nutshell, stated that his brother António had died that very morning in America. It was a classic example of the "knock on the door" by the mailman bringing devastating news which change the course of lives forever in an instant.

It was only several days later that José took it upon himself to tell me the sad news. *Preciso de falar contigo. Senta-te. Teu pai não volta mais da América. Morreu.* (I need to speak with you. Sit down. Your father is not returning from America. He died.) And, as I began to cry realizing that I would never see him again, and some of the immediate implications of the devastating news that I had just heard, I was told: *Um homem não chora.* (A man does not cry.) *Limpa os olhos.* (Dry up your eyes.) Harsh words for a "man" who actually was just a boy. No comforting hug or some kind words from this adult for the grieving boy who had just lost his father and whose natural reaction was to cry about it. And that is how I found out that my dad had disappeared from the face of the Earth.

Inescapably, almost immediately after that day I began to notice little, and not so little, changes in the way that my father's adult friends and neighbors treated me. A nine-year-old may not have yet all his thought processes developed, but he can certainly sense changes in attitude in those around him. Some of these were not so subtle.

For instance, our neighbor José Raposo whom I admired as an accomplished kite maker, and who had recently made the most beautiful kite for me as a birthday gift, a man I addressed all the time as just José Raposo, even though he was an adult simply because I considered him a kind man and my father's friend, at the first social opportunity that came up after António's passing, he made it a point of correcting me by saying that he was not just José Raposo but rather *Senhor* José Raposo, that is to say, *Mr.* José Raposo. I was, of course, embarrassed to be put in my place but then realized that he had simply not had the fortitude to correct me in front of my father. So, instead of stepping in and providing some emotional and moral support to a vulnerable child at a time when he was emotionally weak, *Mr.* José Raposo chose that precise moment to put up a barrier between himself and that hapless boy. The pompous fool felt that he had to assert his authority and let me know that the previous familiarity that I had displayed when addressing him was henceforth totally unacceptable. As a result of the man's new attitude towards me, it became crystal clear to me that all along *Mr.* José Raposo had considered it disrespectful but that his cowardice had prevented him from saying something about it in front of my father. It did not take long after this put down for me to begin understanding that appearances are indeed deceiving when it comes to adults' behavior and that they, when everything is said and done, cannot be totally trusted. And, if you were naïve enough to trust them in the first place, you did so at your own peril because you risked being disappointed and hurt in the process. I was beginning to discover the hypocritical side in adults.

Concerning my uncle José, an insecure man who was dominated by his mother, and who suffered from an inferiority complex vis-à-vis his oldest brother, which led to feelings of resentment and jealousy, he did not wait long either before he, too, showed his true colors; he kicked out of the Machado family home, at his mother's instigation, my mother forcing her to return to her own parents' house, one that she had left fourteen years earlier when she had married António. One would think that José, the youngest of four Machado siblings, left fatherless himself at the age of three, would have been more compassionate and caring regarding the widow and her son but, unfortunately, that was not the case. Instead, he let himself be manipulated by those around him, especially by his mother who had never accepted Elzira as the wife of her firstborn.

For Elzira, it was a move that she was obliged to make out of pure necessity because she had become the target of daily verbal abuse by José and her mother-in-law. Sibling rivalry and jealousy are indeed destructive forces that pull families apart. They shine light on the fragility of human relationships. And, when they are fueled by parents, they have the potential of causing catastrophic results for the survival of the family unit.

Inevitably, if one starts looking closely at most family dynamics being displayed everywhere in the world, one starts noticing all sorts of rifts that at first glance may not be so obvious but that, with time, become quite evident to any attentive observer; sometimes they fester and lead to hate which, in turn, may even lead in some extreme cases to bloody murder.

Louise Penny, in her wonderful murder-mystery novels featuring Chief Inspector Armand Gamache, of the Sûreté du Québec (Québec's

Police Force), his family members, close neighbors and, of course, the criminal element in society, cites frequently one of her favorite poets, W. H. Auden. He says in one of his poems: "And the crack in the teacup opens / A lane to the land of the dead."

It did not take long after António's death for the Machado family to collapse and fall apart. Figuratively, it was just like a fragile teacup that breaks into a thousand pieces when it accidentally drops from one's hand and hits the floor.

3

António's Youth

So, what do we know about this man called António Augusto Machado? He was the oldest of four children, three boys and one girl, aged between three and thirteen, when their father, Manuel Augusto Cristiano Machado, passed away mysteriously in Africa at the young age of thirty-five where he had gone to work as an engineer in the construction of a hydro-electric power station in Lobito, Angola, one of the former Portuguese colonies in that continent. No official explanation was given to his widow and family by the Portuguese government as to what caused his premature death and the circumstances surrounding it. António was thirteen years old when he received the crushing news of his father's passing. He was attending high school and, in the turmoil that ensued this unfortunate turn of events, he faced uncertain times looking forward.

What was going to become of his mother, his three siblings named Manuel (better known as Cristiano), Aida da Conceição, and José, aged 6, 5 and 3 respectively, and of himself, aged 13? What about his own aspirations and dreams? His mother, Maria Eulália do Carmo Machado was, it goes without saying, emotionally destroyed by the news. She was only thirty-three years old. As most women born at the end of the XIX century, she was born in 1897, in Ponta Delgada, she did not have much education and this meant that she was financially vulnerable; in other words, she would have no means of earning a living and of supporting her young family. Consequently, to survive, she would have to rely on the generosity of relatives. Fortunately for her, those relatives did have some financial means and they did do the right thing by coming to the rescue of the widow in distress and her children.

António's grandfather, on his father's side, a man by the name of António Machado Barbosa, together with his own father, Christiano Augusto de Souza, both of whom were carpenters, supported them all until their own deaths in 1937 and 1945, respectively. Luckily, these two gentlemen possessed some investments, a couple of houses and a bit of land. Thanks to them, the family managed to make ends meet and even find the necessary financial resources to keep young António in high school. For the time being, he would continue with his education and his brothers and sister, God willing, would follow suit if tragedy did not knock at their door once again.

But after a terrible blow as the one that had just occurred, daily life is turned upside down. Consequently, as the next few years came and went, António's school marks started to suffer. This becomes evident when one looks closely at his Caderno Escolar – Instrução Secundária, an official record book of a student's marks, attendance and general progress, issued by the high school at the beginning of his or her studies and which is carefully kept at the school's office until the student either completes them or drops out of school altogether. It is a precious document in that it tells a story. In it, one can see that António's many absences lead him to failure in year three. He drops out of school. In the next school year, he attempts a comeback and manages to pass and moves on to year four, which he also completes successfully. Enrolled in year five, he plays truant once again and never finishes his program of studies. In the meantime, though, at least on paper, António continued to be a high school student at Liceu Central de Antero do Quental. However, he was expected to help out financially at home since he was going to be eighteen years old in September of 1935. Very soon a final decision would have to be made by this young man with regards to his education. It came that spring. He quit high school altogether. All in all, he managed to complete four years out of the seven which made up the high school program in those days.

Thus, probably because he had to find work to help out his mother and younger siblings, he was not capable to finish his high school education, a regret that he carried with him for the rest of his life and a professional handicap that prevented him from getting promotions as a public servant with the Regional Government of the Azores.

He was smart and ambitious but, regrettably, lacked the diplomas or degrees that would have carried him far in the domain of public administration. This is the reason that prompted him, I am sure, to specify in his brief business notes left to his wife before his trip in 1961 to the US, that he expected her to do all she could to see to it that their son would be given the chance to go on to higher education, an opportunity which he perceived as unlocking a world of unlimited possibilities, both personal and professional. In the notes left for Elzira, he writes: *Espero que faças toda a diligência para que o Roberto tire un Curso Superior.* (I hope that you do all in your power so that Roberto graduates from university.) He deliberately wrote the last two words of this short sentence with an uppercase *C* and *S*.

What cannot be gleaned from the documentation that I possess is what kind of relationship existed between António and his siblings as they were growing up fatherless. Were they emotionally supportive of one another in the face of adversity? Did they care about each other? Were they friends? One can only speculate about what life would have been like in the Machado household without any of the main protagonists left alive to provide some insight about it. In any case, the way they interacted with one another as mature adults suggests that their commonalities were less important than the differences that separated them. Let's just say that it seems that their family life was not governed by friendship and much less love. And judging from the events that took place in 1960-1961, it looks like that Maria Eulália, their mother, had become by then a bitter woman, a personality trait that comes to light by her indirect involvement in kicking out of the Machado residence my mother and me shortly after my father's passing. My father died in August and by late September the two of us had been shown the door of the house where I was born and my mother had lived for the last fourteen years. I said her "indirect involvement" because she used her youngest son, José, to do the dirty work for her. Her bitterness can be explained partially by the following life events: her husband had passed away relatively young leaving behind four young children, her youngest son had left to Canada in 1957 and, upon returning to São Miguel a few months later, departed again with his wife and son to Cabo Verde, Cape Verde, an archipelago off Africa belonging to Portugal, for a couple of years to establish there a Radio Marconi station, her firstborn had just died and, if that were not enough, her second son, Cristiano, his wife and their three sons were getting set to emigrate to Brazil. On top of all this, Aida and her entire family were living in 1961 in another island, Santa Maria, where her husband, Henrique, was in charge of running the local city hall in Vila do Porto. Her immediate family was falling apart before her very eyes and I suggest that she was to be blamed for it because she had actively promoted sibling rivalry amongst them for years. While they were too busy arguing and fighting among themselves, she could impose her will and authority and rule easily over them all. Divide and conquer. A most effective strategy that has been used for centuries not only by so-called powerful people, especially dictators, emperors, kings, popes, politicians of all stripes, etc., but also by common folk such as parents in their households where they reign supreme if their plan is well executed.

4

A Young Man Goes to Work

António's decision to join the workforce was almost predictable. He simply did not have a choice in the matter out of a sense of responsibility and moral obligation towards his mother and siblings. So, at the age of eighteen, he starts working. That said, what kind of work did he actually do? The documents left behind are silent about his activities and, between the ages of eighteen and twenty-two, we know next to nothing about his professional life. Nevertheless, what we do know for sure is that he was excused from mandatory military service because he was the sole breadwinner in the family.

His true professional activities come to light in 1939. He is twenty-two years old now and has landed a job with Posto de Sanidade Vegetal, which is part of Estação Agrária, a department of the local Regional Government dealing with agriculture. He is given a probationary contract and starts earning a reasonable salary which allows him to lead a decent middle-class life. Soon afterwards, his superiors take notice of the fact that he is a serious-minded young man who wants to succeed in life. He is issued a permanent contract as a civil servant which literally allows him to establish himself professionally and flourish in the next few years.

Physically, he has become a good-looking young man of refined taste. He has nice clothes and starts collecting personal objects of value. He also has become a chain smoker, a nasty habit picked up by so many men of his and subsequent Azorean generations, usually in their teenage years, who regarded it as the most natural thing to do either privately or in public. They were totally unaware of the connection between the vice and heart disease. All sorts of people, both socially and at work, enjoy his company on account of his competence, his good nature and friendliness.

At Estação Agrária, he is well regarded by his immediate superiors who praise the quality of his work on a regular basis and give him more responsibilities as time goes on which, in turn, come with modest salary increases. On February 11, 1943, the Portuguese Government issues him a Diploma de Funções Públicas (Civil Service Diploma). António has not been wasting his spare time; he has been preparing for the mandatory civil service examination.

Shortly afterwards, he is transferred from Estação Agrária to Governo Civil do Distrito Autónomo de Ponta Delgada (Civil Government of the Autonomous District of Ponta Delgada.) The Governo Civil, for short, had moved in 1832 to the old Convento da Conceição (Conceição Convent), a beautiful baroque structure dating back to the XVII century and renamed Palácio da Conceição, where António enjoys a spacious office facing a public garden called Mártires da Pátria (Fatherland Martyrs). He excels at his new job. The president of Comissão Reguladora de Abastecimento de Subsistências, a government Commission in charge of providing supplies, Mr. Victor Machado de Faria e Maia, in the first of several letters written between 1944 and 1948, this one written on December 30th, 1944, says the following:

SERVIÇO DA REPÚBLICA
Ponta Delgada, 30 de Dezembro de 1944
Ao Ex.mo Sr. António Augusto Machado

A Comissão da minha Presidência encarrega-me de comunicar a V. Exa. que, em sua reunião de 29 do corrente, louvou V. Exa. pelos serviços prestados como Encarregado da Secretaria desta Comissão.
Apresento a V. Exa. os meus cumprimentos.
A bem da Nação
O Presidente da Comissão,
Victor Machado de Faria e Maia

(The Committee under my Presidency entrusts me with communicating to you that, in its meeting of the 29th of the current month, it praised you for the services rendered as the person in charge of the office of this Committee.
Please accept my regards.
For the Good of the Nation
The Committee's President,
Victor Machado de Faria e Maia)

In yet another official letter from Governo Civil, dated July 28th, 1948, which I transcribe in its entirety, one reads the following:

SERVIÇO DA REPÚBLICA
Ponta Delgada, 28 de Julho de 1948

Ex.mo Sr.
António Augusto Machado
Ponta Delgada

Sua Exa o Governador Substituto encarrega-me de comunicar a V. Exa que, por seu despacho de 25 do corrente, louvou V. Exa, como encarregado dos serviços da secretaria da Comissão Distrital Reguladora de Abastecimento [d]e Substâncias, há pouco extinta, pelo zelo, dedicação e honestidade com que sempre serviu naquela Comissão, tornando-se por isso um precioso auxiliar.

Apresento a V. Exa. os meus cumprimentos.
A bem da Nação.
No impedimento do Exmo Secretário do
Governo Civil, o Oficial,
João César de Medeiros

(His Excellency the Substitute Governor charges me to communicate to you that, by his dispatch of the 25th of the current month, he praised you as the civil servant in charge of the services of the office of the District's Committee responsible for the Supply of Substances, which ended recently, for the zeal, dedication and honesty with which you always served in the said Committee becoming, as a result, a precious supporter.
Please accept my regards.
For the Good of the Nation.
In the Impediment of the Secretary of the
Civil Government, the Officer,
(João César de Medeiros))

One could not ask for a better reference letter. And, according to Cadastro Geral dos Funcionários Públicos, an official record of his service within the public service sector, there are entries that show that he was praised time and time again for the excellent quality of his work, as well as for his sense of responsibility and loyalty; some of them are signed by the governor himself on several occasions. Here is one that drives this point home:

GOVERNO CIVIL DO DISTRITO AUTÓNOMO DE PONTA
DELGADA
ORDEM DE SERVIÇO No. 9
Louvo o funcionário da Junta Geral em serviço neste Governo Civil, ANTÓNIO AUGUSTO MACHADO, que, durante muiros anos, tem desempenhado, com a maior honestidade, e proficiência, as funções de

encarregado do abastecimento de subsistências, no exercício das quais revelou sempre a maior dedicação e zelo, conduzindo-se por forma a mer[s]ecer, mesmo em delicadas e difíceis situações, a consideração e a estima dos seus superiores hierárquicos, bem como daqueles com quem teve de estar em contacto.
Governo Civil do distrito autónomo de Ponta Delgada, 23 de Novembro de 1954.
O Governador do distrito
Aniceto António dos Santos

(I commend the civil servant of the Administrative Junta, ANTÓNIO AUGUSTO MACHADO, who, for many years, has discharged, with the utmost honesty, and proficiency, the functions of the bureaucrat in charge of the supply of substances, during which he always revealed the greatest dedication and zeal, conducting himself in a way to deserve, even in delicate and difficult situations, the respect and the esteem of his hierarchical superiors, as well as those of the people with whom he had to deal.
Civil Government of the Autonomous District of Ponta Delgada, November 23rd, 1954.
The District's Governor
Aniceto António dos Santos)

It seems that António was able to develop a close professional relationship with this particular governor, one that extended also into the area of personal friendship. Professionally, António was chosen for all sorts of special projects as needed by him. Personally, in turn, when Mr. Aniceto António dos Santos finished his tour of duty in São Miguel, António organized a farewell party for him attended by all the bureaucrats who had served under his administration for which he was most thankful. And, quite a few years later, in 1963, the former governor was still remembering António by name in a newspaper article written for one of Lisbon's newspapers. True friendships do last forever.

So, as a result of his abilities, seriousness and zeal, he was called upon to serve on committees for special occasions that occurred from time to time, such as a visit from an important politician from mainland Portugal, the one of Visita Presidencial ao Distrito de Ponta Delgada (Presidential Visit to the District of Ponta Delgada) by the Presidente da República (President of the Republic), General Craveiro Lopes, on July 21st, 1957, comes to mind, or to serve on ones established to deal with local events and needs as they arose.

Also, in 1952, he was dispatched to the island of Madeira, an island off the coast of North Africa that, together with the island of Porto Santo, make up the Madeira archipelago, and that is today, like the Azores, an autonomous region of Portugal, on official government business to investigate all aspects of the successful local wicker industry in view of establishing a similar one in São Miguel on account of the high unemployment rate facing unskilled workers in the island at the time. I came across an article entitled *A Obra de Vimes* (Wicker Works), written in Lisbon on January 20th, 1963, quite a few years later, in which the former Governador Civil da Região Autónoma dos Açores, Mr. Aniceto dos Santos, recalls António's role in the enterprise. He states:

> *Para o ensino da arte de manufacturar precisávamos de técnicos. Lembrei-me, então, de enviar à Madeira o malogrado António Augusto Machado, inesquecível cooperador e dedicado funcionário que àquela Ilha foi, incumbido de contratar especialistas que viessem para S. Miguel ensinar, ao mesmo tempo que procuraria inteirar-se da orgânica e desenvolvimento da indústria, como se sabe, ali grandemente desenvolvida.*

(For the purpose of teaching the art of manufacturing [wicker] we needed technicians. I remembered, then, to send to Madeira the unlucky António Augusto Machado, an unforgettable collaborator and devoted public servant who went to that Island, entrusted with contacting specialists who would come to São Miguel to demonstrate how it is done, and to try, at the same time, to understand the internal organization and the development of that industry, as everyone knows, greatly developed there.)

All in all, one is left with the distinct impression that António was a superior public servant who, had he possessed a degree from an institution of higher learning, such as Universidade de Coimbra, the most famous one at the time in Portugal, he would have gone places within government circles. That, however, was not the case and, consequently, in the late 1950s, he turned his attention to the world of private enterprise to supplement his income and, therefore, improve his standard of living and lifestyle. Simply put, António had come to the realization that his modest job within the local government and the salary that came with it were not enough to satisfy his desire to succeed financially and socially. He was an ambitious man.

In a letter officially entitled Ordem de Serviço No. 5 (Service Order No. 5) from the departing Governor, Mr. Carlos José Botelho de Paiva, dated February 7th, 1959, there is a reference to António's salary: it was 1 500$00 *escudos* (the Portuguese monetary unit at the time) paid every three months. It was a decent but rather modest salary. As a result, by the time that the Governor wrote that note, António had turned his attention and talents on a part-time basis to the world of private business, a decision that eventually took him twice to America. But, more about this important and critical aspect of his life in another chapter.

Also, I submit to you that he was bored at work and saw no way of advancing within the public sector any further; he had reached the end of the rope in his position with Governo Civil. Therefore, he started looking elsewhere for an escape to his daily routine. And, since so many people that he knew had emigrated to America and done well, he contemplated the possibility of doing the same and starting all over again in a country whose language was so different from his own and where people with his qualifications and level of expertise, upon arrival, were relegated, on account of their lack of fluency in English, to work in factories or in all sorts of menial jobs that required very little, if any, previously acquired skills or training. Let's face it, he had been for most of his adult life a civil servant and had no background in any trade whatsoever. Was he psychologically prepared to face a new harsh reality at the age of forty-two? It is doubtful whether he clearly understood the many difficulties that immigrants face in a new country starting, of course, with the most obvious one, discrimination, even in countries full of immigrants such as the US or Canada.

Most *micaelenses*, as people from São Miguel are called, who emigrated to all parts of the world, especially to the US, Canada, France and Brazil, possessed very little education. Some of them, the lucky few, had a trade which would allow them to work in construction in their new destination. If they were good at it, they could make a decent wage and have a lifestyle that would never have been possible back home. Those were the fortunate ones who bought a house and a car within a few years of having arrived in the new country. As for the women who accompanied these men in this personal adventure, they possessed even less education than their husbands and usually ended up working in factories, went into the house cleaning business, or stayed home to take care of their young children.

Hopefully, the next generation, if encouraged by these humble parents, would complete high school and attend college or university which would open the doors to a professional life and less discrimination. Sadly, the children of the first waves of immigrants did not pursue education beyond elementary or high school and that meant that they were more or less stuck in the same types of jobs that their parents had managed to find upon arrival. Their parents simply did not provide the financial and intellectual support for this necessary next step to take place in the evolution of the Portuguese communities abroad. Education was not a priority for them because they themselves lacked it in their native country.

Although this state of affairs has changed progressively over the decades, the pace of change has been too slow if one takes into account that these families first started arriving in considerable numbers in their adopted countries more than a hundred years ago. Since most of the first wave of immigrants from the Azores had a poor command of Portuguese, and many of the women were, for all intents and purposes, illiterate, it is not surprising that their children were quickly assimilated; indeed, within a few years of living in their new country they could not understand spoken Portuguese and much less read and write in it.

Furthermore, many of them were so uncomfortable with their Azorean background, on account of their parents' perceived lack of social standing, that they went so far as to take concrete steps to anglicize their given and family names in order not to be mistaken for the sons and daughters of recent immigrants. Only the few privileged ones whose parents felt comfortable in both cultures and who returned periodically to their place of origin with them did not suffer some sort of inferiority complex vis-à-vis the anglophone or francophone majorities. Regrettably, even to this day, if one says that one has an Azorean background in the US, Canada, France, Germany and elsewhere, the natives perceive the individual as uneducated and certainly not as competent professionals even if they have the necessary qualifications for the jobs that they hold. A stigma that is most difficult to erase and that can only be wiped out with more education and the passage of time.

In any case, one is left to wonder how António would have dealt with the discrimination inherent in immigration just in order to have a better material life in the US than the one he already enjoyed in São Miguel.

5

At Thirty, António Gets Married

Together with his professional and social successes, somewhere along the line António found love, too. He fell in love with a twenty-one-year-old beautiful woman by the name of Elzira. Their courtship lasted just a couple of years. It seems to have started in 1945. António, being seven years older than her, would have been twenty-eight years old at the time. On December 21st, 1947, they got married. The photographs of the wedding celebration show us a couple that for the next thirteen years, on their wedding anniversary, without exception, went to a professional photographer to record the occasion. And, after my birth in 1952, this tradition continued with one difference; instead of just the two of them in the photographs, now three can be seen. These beautiful pictures were taken by a very talented photographer and artist known to the locals as simply Nóbrega, his given name was Gilberto, famous in São Miguel as well as throughout the Azorean archipelago and the diaspora. The man was much more than a simple photographer, he was an artist. Born in Funchal, Madeira, he arrived in Ponta Delgada in 1942 and by 1943 he had opened a studio called Foto Nóbrega. From the 1940s to the late 1970s the studio was so popular that customers had to make an appointment to have their photograph taken by Mr. Nóbrega. But Mr. Nóbrega was not just interested in taking pictures at important occasions in people's lives such as baptisms, communions and weddings. He also photographed important and unique events as they happened in the Azores. The annual Festas do Senhor Santo Cristo dos Milagres and the volcanic eruption at Capelinhos, just offshore the island of Faial in 1957, come to mind, among many others for which he produced lovely postcards. Foto Nóbrega, unfortunately, closed its doors in 2018; it had been under the management of one of his two daughters ever since his death. The studio had run its course. Most people nowadays take photographs with a cell phone and don't even bother to print them. Fortunately, his collection of tens of thousands of negatives is in the process of being digitalized, albeit slowly, for the enjoyment of future generations of *açorianos* (Azoreans), as people from the Azores are called, not to mention photography lovers everywhere.

Going forward, the newlyweds would be living in the Machado home located on Rua da Boa Nova where António's mother and two of his unmarried siblings also lived. The house would get more and more crowded within the next few years as they, in turn, got married and started having children of their own. This kind of arrangement upon getting married was not at all uncommon in those days in São Miguel, especially in bigger homes that could accommodate several generations. However, living in close contact with one another on a daily basis can bring about rifts amongst family members. Consequently, it did not take long before Elzira felt generally unwelcomed in the Machado residence and she felt that way because she could sense that she was disliked by her mother-in-law. She was not what the old matriarch had in mind for her firstborn. It came down to a personality clash that would become more and more noticeable as the years came and went.

What is not revealed anywhere in the documentation left behind by my mother is whether my father had any other girlfriend before herself. It would be hard to think that such a dashing, elegant young man who related easily to people, would not be sought after by the single women of Ponta Delgada of the late 1930s and throughout the 1940s. Let's face it, at a time and place when there weren't many social and cultural distractions of any kind for young people, what else was there for them to do except date thinking of possible marriage, of course, since dating for the sake of dating would have been discouraged by most parents?

Accordingly, I am inclined to believe that there was some sort of a relationship between himself and a certain Laura da Ponte, a neighbor, two years younger than Elzira, and known to António's mother and his other siblings, especially his sister. She was fair-skinned, blond, with blue eyes, and quite attractive, it seems. She had few of the physical traits of the typical Azorean woman. In brief, she stood out. So, naturally, other women were jealous of her physical beauty and her outgoing personality. She also had other characteristics that many of them did not possess: confidence and flair which made them resent her even more. It did not take long before the gossipers started to characterize her as being an "easy" woman. True or false? Jealousy distorts reality and it has ruined many women's stellar reputations over the ages. From the looks of it, in any case, Laura seems to have been in a vulnerable position as a young woman on account of her family being relatively poor and, believe it or not, because of her natural beauty. In short, for Laura, António would have been a good catch. For him, however, she represented perhaps spoiled goods and, therefore, was not good enough to be his wife and much less the mother of his children. In other words, he was looking for a conformist, not a rebel, and this is possibly the reason why he settled on Elzira when he thought of getting married; for her, he was the husband of her dreams, someone who would offer her a social life and a level of material comfort that otherwise would just be inaccessible.

What is known for certain is that when all three Machado brothers decided to get married, none of them chose Laura. In the mid-1940s, they would have been in their late twenties, certainly António, or their early twenties or late teens, in the case of his two younger brothers. From the pictures that I have in my possession, I can assure you that all three were stylish young men, who enjoyed a sense of entitlement due to their family background and, in my humble opinion, any one of them would have been capable of taking full advantage of a young neighborhood teenager who frequented their house on a regular basis. All three of them, given the opportunity, would not have hesitated in doing so. It would have been the manly thing to do. I explain.

In the 1940s, in Ponta Delgada, as young men, they would have been socially conditioned to exploit the situation unless, of course, they were not *macho* enough, which was certainly not the case for any of them. Consequently, if all the previous assertions are true, Laura's reputation would have been compromised and she would have been considered damaged goods with no bright future in a small city such as Ponta Delgada. No self-respecting man would want her for a wife and much less for the mother of his children, which was the future reserved for most Azorean women of those days.

Indeed, in a small-town society totally dominated by men and where women lacked education and, therefore, access to financial independence, the options were rather limited for them: they either became housewives or spinsters. Very few attended high school after completing mandatory elementary school. Many of them were practically illiterate. Therefore, the dream for most young women was to find a suitable husband who would take care of them financially for the rest of their lives. For the men, these women were a combination of a maid, someone who cleaned their house, prepared their meals, washed their clothes, a partner who took care of their sexual needs, and a mother figure who eventually bore them a few children. Emotionally, many couples were not close, and it was not unusual for men, especially successful ones, who happened to be sexually frustrated by the lack of libido shown by their wives, to have extramarital affairs. In fact, having a lover was perceived by other men with lesser financial means as a sign of prosperity and success and, therefore, something to be admired and even envied.

What is also known for sure, however, is that at one moment Laura marries an older American of Azorean descent by the name of Eneval Jesse (António refers to him by the Portuguese name of Aníbal in his correspondence with Laura) who had returned to São Miguel in search of a young bride and, perhaps, love, too. When this occurred in the late

1940s, he would have been in his late fifties and Laura in her early twenties and in 1960, during António's first trip to the US, he was already seventy years old and Laura thirty-four. Irrespective of the age difference between the two of them, for a young woman without a future in São Miguel this golden opportunity could not be overlooked and she took full advantage of it. She left for Boston where she gave birth to a son shortly afterwards. The couple named him Walter although António, refers to the boy as Val in his business letters.

Ten years after my parents got married, in 1957, when I was five years old, Laura visited São Miguel in the company of her own son who was at least a couple of years older than me. They stayed with friends who lived close to the Machado dwelling. That said, there is no evidence to suggest that António and Laura reconnected emotionally during this particular visit.

In any case, we pick up her trace again in 1960, when António visits the US for the first time. During his brief stay in America, he quickly realized that he needed the services of an interpreter when dealing with American businessmen given his mediocre knowledge of English. So, probably *juntou-se o útil ao agradável*, that is to say, whatever arrangement that was agreed upon by the two of them would combine business with pleasure and add spice to their relationship and their individual lives. Also, by 1960, at the age of forty-two, António was going through a so-called mid-life crisis. The fact that another woman aside from his wife still found him attractive inevitably got to his head. Most men are vain creatures and a bit of flattery from sexy women is more than sufficient to make them fall for them. During the balance of 1960 and all the way to August 15th, 1961, a lot of correspondence, official and personal, was exchanged back and forth between the two of them.

In short, the fact that this relationship rekindled so fast leads one to consider the possibility that perhaps there had been something in the past that united these two people. And, according to Eduarda, Elzira's younger sister, the woman in question was not only a neighbor but also a steady visitor at the family home and that all three brothers were interested in her. However, one has to take her words with a grain of salt as she was jealous of Laura on account of her beauty, confidence and strong personality, attributes that she herself did not possess. The same Eduarda also claims that António was Laura's favorite. This, she confided in me during our several conversations about the time period in question. Her opinion, however, warrants the question: How much did she really know about the goings-on in the Machado household when she herself did not live there at the time?

To sum up, in spite of conflicts in the Machado residence from time to time, generally speaking life was good for the first few years of the newlyweds but, would it last? As Nana Mouskouri's famous song goes: « *Plaisir d'amour ne dure qu'un moment/ Chagrin d'amour dure toute la vie.* »

6

Elzira's Early Years

Elzira was born on April 13th, 1924. She was the eldest of four children, two boys and two girls. Her mother, Margarida de Viveiros, was born on November 27th, 1906, in Ponta Delgada, and her father, Virgínio de Faria, came into this world on November 9th, 1902, in a village called Capelas, on the north side of São Miguel. He was the second of two boys. His brother, Jaime de Faria, was born in 1900. Margarida was a kind woman who never had a chance to attend elementary school and, as a result, was illiterate. She came from a poor family. Her father, António de Viveiros, was a laborer and her mother, Maria da Conceição, was a simple housewife. Virgínio and Margarida got married on February 10, 1923, when she was only seventeen years old. One year later, at the age of eighteen, she gave birth to Elzira. Her husband was twenty-two. The least that can be said about her is that she was verbally and physically victimized by her husband all her married life; he ruled over the growing family as a mini-tyrant. Virgínio, on the other hand, had elementary school education and owned a taxi. Throughout my youth, the car that I associate with him and also the last one that he owned was a 1946 Vauxhall 14-6, which he sold on January 22nd, 1970, together with the license to operate it, for the sum of 80 000$00 *escudos*. He was sixty-seven at the time and had just failed in November of 1969 an eye test which, for all intents and purposes, put an end to his livelihood. For a man who had been in the profession for over forty-five years, having to give it up must have been traumatic. He lost his purpose in life and, within three years, he was dead. It's interesting to note that although this man was a despot at home, as a *chauffeur*, he was well respected by his peers to the point of being named officially their representative when dealing with the local authorities. It was an important role at a time when taxi drivers did not belong to a union. He knew São Miguel like the palm of his hands and, consequently, was sought after when tourists came to visit the island in spite of his lack of knowledge of any language except Portuguese. He was proud of the fact that his island was beautiful and considered it an honor to show its most interesting spots to adventurous tourists, usually people who were visiting São Miguel mostly from Germany, England and France.

Elzira, being the oldest of four children, was only able to complete elementary school. Afterwards, she had to stay home to help her mother with household chores and the care of her three siblings who were respectively seven, five and three years old. She had the brains and the motivation to go further in her schooling if only she had been given a chance. That said, in Virgínio's household education, especially for girls, was not a priority. Her two brothers and younger sister were luckier than her as they were able to attend a vocational high school. One, Francisco, born in 1928, in due time joined the army finishing his career as captain after tours of duty in Moçambique, Angola (two), and Guiné-Bissau, where in the 1960s there was a guerilla war of attrition going on between Portugal and the local populations, one that Portugal could not possibly win after four centuries in Africa without doing much for the economic development of its colonies and even less for the social integration of the indigenous people who were mercilessly exploited and who lived mostly in abject poverty. The other, João, the youngest of the four children, became a *torneiro mecânico*, a lathe technician, at the local Fábrica do Açúcar (Sugar Factory) in Ponta Delgada and, later on, emigrated with his wife to Canada in the mid-1960s. He was my favorite uncle because he was the most fun to be with on account perhaps of being the youngest and because of his jovial disposition. He was born in 1933 which means that in the mid-1950s he would have been in his early twenties and me a mere toddler. As for Elzira's younger sister, Eduarda, whom I have referenced before, after completing most of her studies in the local vocational school, she, in turn, also stayed home to help out her mother and brothers until she got married to António's youngest brother, José, the same man that broke the news to me regarding my father's passing.

As pointed out before, many women in São Miguel in the 1940s and even in the 1950s did not have much education and did not work outside of the home. After completing basic studies and, for the lucky ones, some studies in a vocational school that would allow them to sew or do embroideries, or learn about home economics, they waited patiently for some man to choose them for marriage. Very few attended the local academic high school. In fact, the women who worked as seamstresses, for example, were perceived by more fortunate ones in the close-knit society of Ponta Delgada as coming from very needy families who had to resort to that vocation because there was no other alternative in order for their families to make ends meet. This state of affairs, of course, made them highly vulnerable to abuse by men who perceived them as inferior beings and mere sex objects. These men would feel threatened in their maleness by well-educated and professional women who could be financially independent. So, invariably, they chose to marry women who were meek and who generally lacked confidence in themselves because they lacked education and were not self-sufficient.

I am inclined to believe, from the correspondence left behind by António and the numerous pictures taken of the couple over the fourteen years of married life, that he loved his wife and cared for her before and after she gave birth to his son. He provided for all the necessities of life and then some. Aside from buying her nice clothes, all sorts of accessories, fine jewelry, exquisite perfume, etc., and to facilitate her housework, a gas stove and a refrigerator, appliances that most households did not possess in the 1950s in Ponta Delgada, he also purchased good quality chinaware and silverware to be used at dinner parties when entertaining family, friends and guests on special occasions. There was even spare money to buy a Philips radio. For himself, António continued to collect some luxury items such as an Omega Seamaster 18-Karat solid gold wristwatch and accompanying bracelet which cost him, when he bought it on April 25th, 1961, a small fortune. A grand total of 11 300$00 *escudos*! He also acquired a camera, an Agfa Solinette II, a pair of Weitwinkel binoculars, both items made in Germany, and the iconic Ray Ban sunglasses from the US. At work, for writing, he used exclusively Parker fountain pens. Life was good!

Having said that, time does take a toll on most love relationships and, when boredom and complacency set in, couples do tend to drift apart. This process of alienation between husband and wife is further sped up if children are involved in the picture because the mother, as the main care giver, will find little time and energy to dedicate to her husband. In the Azores of the 1940s, 1950s and even 1960s, it was usually the men who started looking elsewhere for intimacy and sexual gratification. Having a lover was not unusual for men with some means and a relatively good social standing. It seems that António was ripe for this lifestyle in 1960. He felt restless and perhaps neglected by his wife and was in the throngs of a mid-life crisis. By this time the couple had been married for thirteen years and, in spite of the most recent trip together to mainland Portugal in the spring of 1960, their love life was in limbo. To make matters worse, Elzira developed a problem with her right knee which had to be put in a cast for several months, impeding greatly her freedom of movement, as the cast went from the foot all the way to just above the knee itself. Needless to say, the couple's busy social life had to be put on hold for the time being, which further complicated matters between husband and wife.

7

Married Life in the Machado Household

As pointed out elsewhere, Elzira had moved into her mother-in-law's home, located at Rua da Boa Nova, when she got married in 1947 and that is often the worst mistake that a newlywed can make. Living with one's in-laws in their home can be an insurmountable challenge for most brides. In Portuguese there is a saying that goes like this: *Quem casa quer casa*. In that language, it's a play on words for the word *casa* can be both a verb and a noun. It simply means that whoever gets married needs a house of his or her own in order for peace to be possible among family members. Sound advice for all those who intend to keep families united as time marches on.

This proverb proved to be true because Elzira experienced all sorts of trouble trying to establish herself in her new abode. At the time, her mother-in-law was fifty-two years old and she was still firmly in charge of all her sons and daughter, especially those who were still single and living with her, Aida and José. By this time Cristiano, the second oldest, was already married; he had married in 1946 at the age of twenty-two and had moved down the street to inhabit another house that belonged to the Machado family where he lived for free. António, the eldest, was perceived as the heir apparent of the family home and, therefore, was seen as a threat by his siblings. The fact that he had sacrificed five years of his youth for their sake was conveniently brushed aside by all of them. They resented his seniority, apparent authority and predominant role in the household and this created friction amongst them.

The occasional clashes did not make life pleasant for the new arrival and, actually, it isolated her from family decisions; instead of welcoming her as a person worthy of respect based on her own merits and qualities, they ostracized her. To complicate matters, Elzira did not display a strong personality and, therefore, could not be forceful enough in imposing herself; this character flaw made life more difficult for her all the while making it easier for them to ignore her. So, soon after moving in, it became clear that the only person that she could count on to defend her was António who, as time marched on, was becoming more and more resented by his other siblings. The knives were being sharpened for a future back stabbing.

As the 1950s drew to an end, António's professional, financial and social successes became more and more evident to all of his siblings and mother. Nevertheless, instead of celebrating his accomplishments because everybody was benefitting directly or indirectly from them, they, instead, were bitter about his rise in status. The destructive feelings of jealousy and envy that they harbored towards António could not be hidden from view any longer and there were frequent disputes between them which made them speak hardly to one another.

The rift among the brothers and sister became accentuated when António decided to make improvements to the house that legally belonged to all of them in the late 1950s. And his mother kept them all divided by continuing to promote sibling rivalry with all sorts of little intrigues of her own making. As previously noted, she was a master manipulator who excelled at playing the innocent victim to perfection after creating unnecessary trouble of her own. In short, she was a troublemaker. The Machado family became a classic example of a dysfunctional family.

By the time that the old matron died in 1965, her oldest son was dead, her second oldest had emigrated to Brazil with all of his family and the youngest one had taken off to Canada, again, after a brief stint there in 1957. Her daughter and her family were the only ones who were still living with her, and they, too, eventually emigrated to the US in the 1970s after Aida's oldest daughter married an American citizen of Azorean descent, Carlos, who happened to have been a close neighbor before his own family emigrated to the US.

Nowadays, because the Machado home was left to Aida by the old matriarch upon her death, only her children will stay in it when on vacation in São Miguel. The Machado family home, which had been a beehive of activity for so many decades, a house that was bursting at the seams with parents, uncles, aunts and cousins throughout the 1950s, now rests empty most of the year. The descendants of António, Cristiano, Aida and José have been dispersed and have put roots elsewhere: in Canada, Brazil, US and Europe and, in any case, in spite of having been raised together as children, none of them are close friends nowadays; they don't keep in touch. The goodness that one seeds is eventually the same that one reaps a thousand-fold. Regrettably, very little or none was seeded by the Machado grandparents and parents of the generation that is still alive today. *C'est la vie!* Such is life!

8

Finally, a Son Is Born

Finally, to add to António and Elzira's joy and happiness, a son was born on August 13th, 1952, at 9:15 at night, weighing 3,500 kilos. The birth took place at home under the supervision of a midwife as was the custom in those days. They named me Roberto Augusto de Faria Christiano Machado. I was a beautiful baby who quickly took over all aspects of their married life. I became their pride and joy. From that moment onwards, in the yearly photograph celebrating the couple's wedding anniversary, one can see me too. In addition, on my birthday, another tradition was established, that of visiting Nóbrega and taking my picture, one that lasted until 1960 when I turned eight years old. 1961, the year that marks my father's passing, saw the end of many wonderful traditions that simply could not be afforded any longer by my mother who was now a widow in distress.

Up to the time that I was born, Elzira had dedicated herself exclusively to making sure that her husband was well taken care of, that is to say that he lacked nothing. However, once a mother, most of her time henceforth was devoted to taking care of her child who, like the vast majority of toddlers, needs and deserves a lot of attention. This new state of affairs, of course, did not mean that she neglected her husband totally. It simply meant that she had less time to cater to some of his emotional and physical needs, that's all. In adopting this attitude, she was very much like most Azorean women of her generation who, after the birth of a child, find a more urgent purpose in their lives.

As an aside, it must be pointed out that after giving birth to several children some women of Elzira's generation were so busy taking care of them that they almost forgot about the existence of their husbands. They, imperceptibly, neglected them leading to the detriment of the relationship that once existed between them. Consequently, some husbands turned to lovers or prostitutes to satisfy their sexual needs and libido. It was not unheard of in the São Miguel of those days for some of these men to father children, accidentally, of course, who would never be accepted by their half brothers and sisters as they were considered illegitimate by the legitimate ones and only referred to in pejorative terms such *filhos de puta*, sons of a whore.

For his part, António loved me dearly. He was proud of me and spoiled me rotten. He showered me with affection and toys and, whenever possible, took me along on social outings with his friends where I was exposed to adult conversations about all sorts of subjects: politics, business, soccer, etc. This, it goes without saying, after I was a bit older. The regular Friday evening trip to Mr. José do Rego's *adega*, a wine cellar, in São Roque, a village nearby, stays vivid in my memory among many others as there I would taste delicious pieces of the famous Queijo de São Jorge, cheese from the island of São Jorge, on slices of *pão de milho*, corn bread, local delicacies, while the adults enjoyed the same but accompanied with a glass of wine. And, on winter Sundays, he took me along to the local soccer stadium, Estádio Jâcome Correia, to enjoy the matches between the local teams. As soccer is the national sport of Portugal, this was definitely a wonderful treat for any young boy. Sunday afternoons in July, August and part of September were spent at the *poças*, natural swimming pools, of the *calhau*, the rocky shore, separating the end of the Machado's backyard from the sea. António, like most Azoreans, loved the sea and enjoyed swimming in the clear and temperate waters of the Atlantic. Toy boats, life buoys, snacks and drinks were brought to the site and all the children had a great time.

It was in one of those natural swimming pools that António taught me how to tread water and, later on, how to swim and dive. All the children who were fortunate enough to live in homes whose backyards faced the *calhau* considered it an extension of their own backyard and spent considerable time there either flying kites or going for swims. It was a marvelous place to meet all sorts of other children from the neighborhood with similar interests. None of us were ever bored. There was always something going on that caught our attention and interest. Sometimes tempers flared and mild conflicts occurred, mostly over kites that had gotten entangled, but these never lasted too long and by the next day were all but forgotten and the fun resumed without animosity between old friends.

As for other toys, there were too many to mention but the one that I most treasured for quite a few years arrived on Christmas Day in 1959 when I was seven years old. It was a beautiful red and yellow bicycle that I had been eyeing in a local shop window for weeks. But, even as early as 1954, there had been a red tricycle, the first toy that afforded me a taste of what it meant to be in control of a rudimentary speed machine. It, too, was enjoyed for many years. And, in between the tricycle and the bicycle there were toy airplanes, a train set, roller skates and hockey sticks, balls of all sizes, story books and puzzles, and the list goes on and on. As pointed out, António did not spare a dime to keep me happy.

In the 1950s, in Ponta Delgada, for any boy or girl under the age of ten years old, there were essentially only three public celebrations noteworthy during the whole year: the first one was Christmas, *Natal*, the second one was the cult of the Senhor Santo Cristo dos Milagres, the Lord Holly Christ of Miracles, a statue of Ecce Homo believed to have been a gift from Pope Paul III, in the XVI century, to a few nuns in São Miguel who went to Rome because they wanted to establish a new convent in the island. The last one was Carnival which enabled the young to put on costumes and attend a few neighborhood parties where goodies were made for the occasion, such as *malassadas*, a type of doughnut, music was played, confetti thrown about, and some dancing for the teenagers occurred. These three festivities were totally different from one another but all demanded a lot of effort and enthusiasm from the local adult population in order to stage them.

Christmas was and continues to be, of course, a favorite with children in many different countries on account of Santa Claus, *Velho do Natal*, who brings gifts on Christmas Eve or on the morning of Christmas Day to all boys and girls who behaved themselves throughout the year. In the Machado residence, he used to show up "in person" (someone dressed as Santa) on the morning of December 25th. But, in Ponta Delgada, the Christmas season used to begin when the merchants decorated their shop windows with all sorts of tempting items a few weeks before the big day. Naturally, sometime before Christmas Day, many parents made it a point of duty to go out with their children after dinner, when the store windows would be lit, to view what was on display and to figure out what particular articles were appealing to their offspring. For the vast majority of the children who seldom went out at night at all, the beautiful toys, games, articles of clothing, etc., all shining on the display cases, made them dream wide awake about what Santa might bring. It was a magical time of the year to walk in the darkened streets in the cool early December evenings where the only lights that shone bright were the ones blazing on the shop windows. Of course, not a single child would ever be satisfied with just one trip to the downtown core of Ponta Delgada at night time. Neither were their parents, for that matter, as they enjoyed window shopping, too.

The religious festivities associated with the image of Senhor Santo Cristo dos Milagres were in those days, and also continue to this day, to be the most important ones of Ponta Delgada and throughout the Azores. They attracted thousands of pilgrims from all over São Miguel, the other islands, and from the Azorean diaspora. Alas, due to COVID-19, the celebrations were cancelled, to the chagrin of many people, for the first time in centuries. The festivities themselves go on for six days and they take place around the 5th Sunday after Easter. Out of the six days, the three most important ones are Saturday, Sunday and

Monday. And, out of the three days, the most solemn one is definitely Sunday. That is when a large procession takes place and the bust of Senhor Santo Cristo dos Milagres is taken from the Convento e Capela de Nossa Senhora da Esperança, the Convent and Chapel of Our Lady of Hope, and carried on its bier along the main streets of downtown Ponta Delgada, which are all covered beforehand with fresh flowers arranged in geometric patterns. The procession itself and the street decorations are a sight to behold. The convent and its adjoining small tower face a public square named Campo de São Francisco, also known as Praça 5 de Outubro, October 5th Square. In the middle of the square there is a kiosk where, at night, different philharmonic bands from across São Miguel take turns playing musical pieces. The façade of the convent and its adjoining small tower are decorated with thousands and thousands of light bulbs, the square itself, the Avenida Marginal and some of the major streets are also adorned with banners and lights that come on at night time and the result is the creation of a wonderland that is enjoyed by people of all ages. Any person from São Miguel, young or old, who has experienced this public event at some point in his or her life, will never forget it because it combines religious fervor with social joy and pride. The impression left in one's memory is so indelible that time cannot erase it and it explains, to a large extent, why *micaelenses* who have established themselves in foreign countries, such as the US or Canada, will at least one more time in their lifetime return to Ponta Delgada to participate in it. Some make it a point of returning every year.

Most local families, it goes without saying, try to look their best for this occasion. So, new clothes are in order for all those who can afford them. For children, it's not so much the religious component that pleases them but rather the fact that all sorts of fun rides such as small roller-coasters and bumper cars, are available in an improvised amusement park of sorts for their merriment. And, if that was not enough, there are also street vendors in and around the Campo de São Francisco, with all sorts of tasty goodies to tempt their palate. Every child under the age of ten is sure to like this particular festival. I was no exception to the rule. I was spoiled rotten at this time of the year by my parents.

Finally, with regards to Carnival, one of the most interesting and unusual traditions was the confection of *limas*, little wax shaped balls filled with water, made by the adults prior to *entrudo*, the three days before Lent, that people threw at passers-bye from their second-floor windows or balconies just for the fun of it. Also, in connection with this tradition, there was another one just for a few very macho young men; they used to get together and pile up on truck beds with *seringas*, watering guns, and proceeded to spray mercilessly all those who dared throw *limas* at them. Most young children were afraid of these antics and only observed cautiously the proceedings from behind a window where they were sure not to be drenched.

All in all, I lived a privileged life and was a very happy boy, one who related easily to other children my own age and made friends quickly. Life was indeed beautiful and worry free. And, there were trips further afield, too. One to the island of Santa Maria in 1958, and another trip to visit the entire archipelago just a few months later, after the eruption of the Vulcão dos Capelinhos (Capelinhos volcano), in the island of Faial. Many of the islands did not have docks and, therefore, passengers had to be transported by *lanchas*, small motor boats, to land, sometimes in rough seas, something that scared me to death. These trips widened his limited horizons and developed in me a love for adventure and traveling. At the same time, although I did not know it at the time, they revealed the unique beauty of the Azores, this miniscule group of nine islands lost in the immense Atlantic, which remain one of the best kept secrets to this day.

I reiterate, António played a major role, even though it was just a brief one, during part of my formative years. Lamentably, he also disappeared from my life at a time when I was going to need him the most for guidance and support during my adolescence and early adulthood. Every adolescent deserves and needs a loving father who will show him how to become a decent man and, possibly, a father one day, too. Luckily for me, when my father disappeared from the scene, my mother stepped in to protect me from all harm and to see to it that her husband's last wishes were carried out in spite of the enormous personal sacrifices required from her. She was a devoted mother who became focused on just one thing: sacrificing everything for me. She was only thirty-seven years old when António passed away and she could have married again if she so had wished, but she never did. I don't think that deep down in her mind any other man compared favorably with António and, thus, she dropped the idea of remarrying altogether if it ever occurred to her in the first place.

9

António's Travel Adventures Outside of São Miguel

As the title of this biography asserts, António was a very proud Azorean. And, like many Azoreans, he loved travelling. Most of them share this characteristic. It's a direct result of what is commonly referred to as *insularidade*; the fact that no matter where one turns in any of the nine islands of the archipelago, one is always surrounded by water and feels isolated and even trapped by this natural barrier that hinders one's freedom of movement. It's like being confined to a cell in a prison. As a consequence, one longs to get away from the confinement inherent in all aspects of daily life and discover new places with vast horizons. Places in which one can travel for days without being blocked by a natural barrier such as an ocean. Escaping from isolation has always been the dream of consecutive generations of Azoreans and, therefore, it has become a leitmotiv in Azorean literature.

The Azores, located in mid-Atlantic, was discovered by a Portuguese navigator, Diogo de Silves, in 1427. Its coordinates are: 30° 30' and 40° N and 25° and 31° 30' W. It is 1,500km from Europe and 4,000km from America. The archipelago consists of nine volcanic islands divided into three groups. The Eastern Group is composed of São Miguel and Santa Maria, the Central one is made up of Terceira, Graciosa, Faial, São Jorge and Pico and, finally, the Western Group has two islands, Flores and

Corvo. The closest island to Europe is Santa Maria and the furthest is Flores. Between Santa Maria and Flores there is a distance of approximately 600km or 336 nautical miles. Given its strategic location, the Americans saw fit to build two air bases in the archipelago, one in Lajes, Terceira, in 1943, and the other one in Santa Maria, in 1944. It goes without saying that the US paid good money to the central Portuguese government in Lisbon for the use of the two airports for many years. As for the Azores itself, it never saw much of that money being reinvested in its own economic development which explains, at least partly, the continued emigration of its population in the 1940s, 1950s and 1960s. Its language is, of course, Portuguese.

São Miguel, the largest island in the archipelago, is 65km in length by 14km in width. Its total land mass is 759,41km². It's also the most populated with about 140,000 people as of 2020. Its capital city, Ponta Delgada, was established in 1518. It had a population of approximately 69,000 inhabitants in 2011. Today, it's by far the most important city of the Azores and its capital. The main campus of the Universidade dos Açores was founded there in 1976.

Given its isolation, and the relative poverty of many of its inhabitants, for many years if not decades, it was natural for quite a few to want to run away to other lands that would offer a better future for themselves and, eventually, God willing, for their families. It was a wish that appealed to their sense of adventure, too.

Accordingly, some of them, the ones involved in the local whaling industry living in Pico and Faial, two islands only 6km apart, left their respective birth places by boarding illegally the American whaling ships that routinely stopped there, when whaling was still allowed in the Atlantic, of course, and made it, after many trials and tribulations, to the "Promised Land", America.

Every once in a while, out of pure desperation, and at the risk of freezing to death in the process, the odd Azorean would also make the news by hanging on to the landing gear of an airplane as it took off from the international airports in Santa Maria or Terceira on its long way to the US. A stowaway! Desperate people will do desperate things if they think that they can improve their lot in life, including paying the ultimate price for it.

Apart from these extraordinary and desperate acts, over the decades, many Azoreans emigrated legally to France, Germany, Brazil, Angola and Mozambique (two former Portuguese colonies in Africa), Venezuela, Hawaii and, of course, the US and Canada where nowadays, in these two last countries, there are huge communities of Azoreans especially in the eastern part of the US and in the province of Ontario, Canada. Literally, the Azorean diaspora is huge given the small population of the archipelago. There are nowadays more Azoreans living outside of the Azores than in the archipelago proper. In spite of facing a myriad of problems in their new destinations, quite a few have improved significantly their standard of living by working hard at whatever comes their way.

Azoreans, generally speaking, are sentimentalists at heart. So, a good many of them, once they have been able to put aside some savings, like to return to their city, town or village to visit family, relatives and friends left behind. Once an Azorean, always an Azorean, no matter where life takes you. So, in their new countries, they experience the blues, what in Portuguese is referred to as *"saudade da terra"*, the longing that they feel to revisit the place of birth even though it may not have been the happiest of places when they actually lived there. As time marches on one does have a tendency of coloring and perceiving one's early years as the best time of one's life in spite of all sorts of personal challenges at that time including, of course, poverty.

As far as one can tell, António's first trip outside of São Miguel took place in 1947; it took him to the closest island to São Miguel called Santa Maria, a mere 57 nautical miles or 85km away from Ponta Delgada. In order to get to his destination, he, together with a few friends, boarded a sailboat called Furnas in its inaugural trip between the two neighboring islands. On the way back, they were somewhat luckier in that they sailed in a small *contratorpedeiro* (destroyer) named Lima. On the reverse side of the photo taken on that special occasion one can read the following note written by António: *Regresso de Santa Maria a bordo do Contratorpedeiro Lima, 3 h e 15 m de viagem em 2 de Maio de 1947.* (Return trip from Santa Maria aboard the destroyer Lima, 3 h and 15 m long on May 2nd, 1947.) This attention to detail can be seen in the short descriptions on the back side of most of the photographs taken by him throughout his lifetime.

The purpose of this trip seems to have been to check out the facilities of the wartime military air base built by the Americans there in 1944. In the late 1950s, this particular air base transformed itself into an international airport for transatlantic flights and, thus, for many Azorean emigrants it played a huge role in their life because it was the point of departure for traveling to the US or Canada in search of a better life. It was a must stopover for airplanes coming from Europe and destined to the Americas. With the passage of time, however, this airport became more or less obsolete with regards to transatlantic flights as jets took over the skies from propeller aircraft and when the new international airport in São Miguel, John Paul II International Airport, was inaugurated in the late 1960s. Nowadays, the international airport in São Miguel is where people travelling to the Azores from the US, Canada or European countries will land before on-going flights to elsewhere in the archipelago. This, of course, makes a lot of sense since most passengers will stay in the island. Santa Maria's airport is now relegated to serving as an air-traffic-control center for north Atlantic flights. Consequently, the island's population has dwindled significantly ever since its glory days in the 1950s.

Once again, in August of 1958 António returned to Santa Maria. This time he was returning there with his wife and young son. He wanted to show them something that they had never seen before, that is to say the most important commercial airport in the entire Azores. So, in order to get to our destination all three of us boarded a ship called Arnel, one that did the runs between the islands of the archipelago on a regular basis. Once there, I was mesmerized by the sheer volume of air traffic and the size of the airplanes. I had never seen anything like it before.

I, who was fascinated by airplanes as a young boy of six, and who had quite a collection of them as toys, thought that I was in paradise when I found himself at Santa Maria's International Airport. Airplane after airplane kept on landing and, after refueling, taking off bound to the Americas or Europe. It was a sight to behold, and it was most entertaining. For a boy who had only seen, every once in a while, a small airplane used by SATA (Sociedade Açoreana de Transportes Aéreos), a De Havilland DH, 104 Dove, at the miniscule Santana airfield in São Miguel, located on the north side of the island and, therefore, not readily accessible to the people of Ponta Delgada on a regular basis, it was a dream come true to watch these huge airplanes; needless to say, once at the airport, airplane watching was the only thing that I wanted to do during the brief visit to the island. It took a lot of convincing and persuasion on my parents' part to make me agree to spend some of the precious time left exploring other places and sights like Vila do Porto, its main town, the picturesque bay of São Lourenço, and Praia Formosa with its lovely white sandy beach which is such an unusual sight in the Azores, one that is only seen in Santa Maria. Eventually, of course, they succeeded at dislodging me from the airport promising to return there as soon as possible.

A couple of months later that same year, António, all three of us also had the opportunity to visit most of the islands in the archipelago. This time we boarded a much bigger ship called Carvalho Araújo on October 21st, 1958, on trip number 1976. It was a round trip between Ponta Delgada, in São Miguel, and Santa Cruz das Flores, in the island of Flores, the most western point of Europe, with ports of call along the way in Terceira, Graciosa, São Jorge, Pico, Faial and Corvo. It was an amazing cruise that lasted about a week.

As time passed, António became more and more convinced that many of the local Azorean products, such as dry fava beans, peas, potatoes, eddoes, chicory, sugar beets, pineapples, canned fish, and others, were of superior quality and, therefore, could be sold not only regionally but also nationally and internationally. He took full advantage of this particular trip throughout the Azores to contact acquaintances in some of the islands who perhaps would be interested in the export business.

As an added bonus for all three of us, it was also an amazing opportunity to discover the natural beauty, diversity and uniqueness of each one of the islands visited. It is said by many tourists that the Azores is one of the best kept secrets in the world, and they are certainly right about that. It's the unspoiled beauty of nature together with the friendliness of the *açorianos* that really makes most tourists want to return to the archipelago time and again. Although I was only six years old at the time, I have kept vivid memories of that unforgettable trip. Islands materializing themselves out of nowhere in the middle of the vast Atlantic is indeed something extraordinary for any person to behold let alone a child of six!

Also, in between these trips, in 1952, António was dispatched by the Governor of the regional government to the island of Madeira to study the feasibility of introducing in São Miguel a new industry, that of wicker works, one that was very well-established in Madeira and that employed hundreds of people, in order to reduce the number of the unemployed and unskilled workers back home who were facing tough times in the early 1950s.

Finally, in May of 1960, my parents took advantage of an organized excursion to mainland Portugal which lasted an entire month. It was a comprehensive tour of the country which included a visit to the religious shrine in Fátima on May 13th. I did not go with them. Although I was left with my maternal grandparents for a month, António did not forget about me and mailed a postcard every single day from the different cities and points of interest that he was passing through. Thus, this unique collection of postcards is not only a wonderful pictorial snapshot of mainland Portugal of 1960, but also an accurate account of his thoughts and feelings as the trip unfolded. Not to mention, of course, the numerous recommendations that he makes to me. Also, while passing through Lisbon, António made it a point of connecting personally with his business acquaintances in the capital. It was an excellent opportunity to put a face to a name.

This particular trip enabled the Machado couple to make new friends. They met Mr. João Bento Soares da Silva and his wife, Mrs. Maria Helena Soares da Silva, who became very close friends over the next few months in spite of being older than António and Elzira. All four of them shared such a great time during the trip that even after António's death the couple kept on visiting my mother periodically to reminisce about that unforgettable trip and tell her of their new travel adventures. True friends do not abandon each other when tragedy strikes. In fact, they become closer in order to cushion the blow to a dear friend caused by a cruel destiny.

All in all, one can certainly state that António had developed by 1960 a taste for travelling that satisfied his sense of adventure and curiosity and which, in turn, opened his eyes and mind to new possibilities when it came to his particular lifestyle. He had become, like many of his fellow countrymen, an explorer. Any person who is born and grows up in an island can relate to the strong desire to just pack up and leave one's place of birth. An islander is somewhat like a prisoner. Both lack freedom of movement. The former is surrounded by water everywhere he looks and turns and the latter faces constantly four walls that remind him, with every short step he takes, that he is not free to do as he pleases. Both long for freedom of movement without any restrictions. An islander, *um ilhéu*, an islet, as we sometimes refer to someone from the Azores, is the luckier of the two, especially if he has some financial resources at his disposal that will afford him the opportunity to take off. The poor inmate has no say concerning his status, he is stuck in a cell and at the mercy of the authorities with regards to his eventual freedom if it ever happens.

10

Finding Business Partners in his Native Island

On a personal level, António was a pleasure to be with because of his many attributes; consequently, he was very well-liked and had many friends. He was popular and respected by colleagues, friends and acquaintances. He was a born leader who organized frequently outings for his co-workers and friends just for the pleasure of relaxing and spending quality time together. These outings took the group into the beautiful countryside, to such places as Sete Cidades, Lagoa do Fogo, Lagoa do Congro, Furnas, Nordeste, and many other places of interest, usually on summer Sundays. They brought with them food and drink and, again, from the pictures left behind, one can tell that there was a lot of friendship and camaraderie among them. In winter, on Sunday afternoons, António attended soccer matches at the Municipal Stadium for which he had a season's pass. These activities allowed him to network with all sorts of locals who, perhaps, like himself, shared a desire to explore the world of private business. That is probably how he met Mr. Dinis Mota Soares, Mr. Manuel Rodrigues Castelo, Mr. Eduardo Valério, Mr. Bento Pavão da Silva, Mr. Mariano Raposo Morgado and Mr. Guilherme Raposo, six gentlemen who were willing to risk thousands of *escudos* to become his business associates in the export of Azorean products. António started out by testing the waters in mainland Portugal itself.

It is interesting to note that his first attempt at exporting a product in large scale from his native São Miguel took place in 1959. The product was potatoes. He found a willing partner in Mr. Dinis Mota Soares. The company that he was dealing with was the Firma Morais e Palhares, with headquarters located at Rua dos Caminhos de Ferro, no. 28, Lisboa. It is also noteworthy to point out that his dealings with this particular company ended up in court in 1961. According to the decision handed down by the court, he had sent 915 bags of potatoes with a total weight of 45,750 Kg and Morais e Palhares had neglected to make the necessary arrangements by opening a credit line at its bank in Lisbon for the deal to be completed. As a result, some of the potatoes had rotten away in Lisbon's port waiting to be delivered. In his case against the company, António was asking to be compensated for the sum of 73 200$00 *escudos* plus the legal interest of 6% associated with the case. Of course, when the court's decision finally came down on November 24th, 1962, António had already passed away. The court awarded my mother the sum of 17 066$20 *escudos*, a far cry from what he was asking for; as such, its decision would have disappointed him tremendously. Perhaps, had he been alive at the time, this particular turn of events would have been a sign that the business world can be a brutal one. But would this initial set-back have been enough to discourage him from pursuing business deals in the future? One can only speculate about such matters.

Almost at the same time that he was looking for possible business partners and market outlets for Azorean products within the borders of Portugal, he started to look for the same in the US where many Azoreans had settled, especially along its eastern coast, in places such as Fall River, Taunton, Providence and, of course, in the Boston area itself and, in particular, Somerville, where his next-door neighbors had put down roots in the late 1950s. In that decade alone, lots of *micaelenses* emigrated to America.

In fact, it is said that between 1921 and 1977, some 250,000 Azoreans established themselves in Massachusetts and Rhode Island alone. That means that by the mid-1950s the steady flow of *açorianos* to the US was well under way and all these individuals were familiar with the different dishes that could be prepared using fava beans, a staple in Azorean cuisine. This group alone was not a negligible market for that specific product. But António was also aware that there were large communities of Italian Americans and Latinos in Boston and New York City who considered the product a staple too. So, when an old acquaintance of his, Mr. João Miranda, returned to São Miguel on a personal holiday in 1956, António invited him and a few friends of his for lunch at the Machado residence. It was January 8th, a date that António would not forget easily going forward because tentative business possibilities were discussed during the meal. If nothing else, Mr. João Miranda could serve as an interpreter, as a go-between, so to speak, between himself and his American counterparts, a role which he did perform during António's first trip to the US in 1960. Here was a fellow islander who had made it in the US on account of his grocery store. He would definitely be a good connection to keep in mind if António were to visit the "land of opportunity". The fact that Mr. João Miranda loved fava beans and other Azorean products solidified in António's mind the feasibility and viability of his project.

But for the North American business adventure, he needed the help of the six men mentioned above due to the amount of money required to get it going. They were all willing partners. The sums of money that they were willing to risk were indeed huge by 1961 standards. Between all of them they invested in the enterprise about 700 000$00 *escudos*! All seven men shared the same dream: that of seeing local products being appreciated, on account of their high quality, and sold in the US. Naturally, along the way they also expected to benefit financially from the venture. They expected to make a profit. That said, out of the seven men only one of them possessed the interpersonal skills and the confidence to deal personally with potential export and import business companies in the US, and that man was António. Therefore, he became their point man.

He also had a trump card up his sleeve that the others did not possess: he knew of acquaintances, friends, and neighbors who had emigrated to America, such as Mr. João Miranda, who had put down roots in Fall River and, therefore, could facilitate the establishment of real business connections with American companies and individuals such as himself willing to import products from São Miguel. That leads one to conclude that António must have been thinking as early as 1956, when he invited his guest for lunch, about exploring the world of private enterprise as a means to supplementing his salary as a bureaucrat. With time, this idea would crystalize in his mind and culminate with the two trips to the US.

António was a meticulous man in everything that he undertook professionally and, therefore, in order to convey the impression to the Americans that he was a serious businessman and not simply an amateur, he ordered from a printing company in Ponta Delgada his own business stationary. So, at the top of each sheet of paper, centrally located, one can find the name António Augusto Machado and, to the left of it, his logo, the *açor*, the Azorean goshawk. It was a deliberate choice on his part. He wanted people to know not only that he was a proud Azorean, but also for them to associate the Azores with the region of Portugal from where the products that he was exporting originated. And, immediately to the right of his name one can see the list of the products in both Portuguese and English that he was promoting. The letterhead was well conceived and executed.

So, by August of 1960 António was more than ready to fly to Boston. During the winter, spring and early summer of that year he had been in close contact with two American companies: the Musolino Lo Conte Co. and the L. N. White Co., and by mid-August the fava beans had been shipped by boat to New York. António was looking forward to meeting personally his American counterparts who were definitely very interested in importing this particular product from São Miguel and paying a reasonable price for it. They had received samples of the product and they were impressed by its superior quality; furthermore, they knew that there would be a market for it, as António had predicted all along to his partners in São Miguel. In conclusion, the future looked promising for the *micaelense* partners and the future of the export enterprise that they had created.

11

António's Business Connections in the US

António having heard countless stories of financial and personal success from Azoreans living in the US and returning on vacation to São Miguel, became convinced that America was indeed a great country with a huge market. Consequently, he actively sought individuals who could help him out in his business export efforts if nothing else by serving as translators or interpreters (in spite of private lessons to learn English, his knowledge of the language was rather limited) and ideally as business partners, too. Given his vast network of friends and acquaintances, both in São Miguel and those established already in the US, he was convinced that his goal would be easily achievable.

So, prior to his first trip to Boston and New York in 1960, he connected with an old acquaintance from São Miguel, the aforementioned Mr. João Miranda who lived in Fall River, and invited him to accompany him to the meetings with the personnel of the two companies that were interested in importing Azorean products. They were: Musolino Lo Conte Co. – Importers & Exporters, with offices in Boston and New York, being managed respectively by Mr. Anthony Lo Conte and Mr. Carl Lo Conte, the L. N. White & Company, Inc. – Import & Export, with headquarters located in New York, under the management of Mr. Larry White, and the S. Giannetto Co. – Food Products of Brooklyn, administered by Mr. S. Giannetto. Of course, Mr. João Miranda accepted willingly António's invitation.

It is also noteworthy that aside from US companies António looked for business opportunities in Europe by contacting the Cairns Export Company, in Wakefield, England, and even the Guido Galimberti & Figli Co. in Venice, Italy, but these proved to be fruitless and a waste of time and effort for him as nothing came of it. Irrespective, with companies in America willing to do business now, and companies clearly interested in Azorean products, especially fava beans which came in two sizes, small or large, and either peeled or unpeeled, António felt that the ground work rested on solid footing for him to move forward with his project. To that end, he booked his flight to the US for August 21st, 1960.

His trip was a success from a personal as well as a business point of view. From a business perspective, he met personally with his American counterparts and was able to put names to faces and figure out personalities. From a personal perspective, he was able to connect with all sorts of friends and acquaintances. Among them was a woman from São Miguel, the aforementioned Laura da Ponte, a woman that at one moment António had known well because she had been a neighbor and a friend of the Machado family. The least that can be said about their future relationship is that the 1960 trip set in motion his reacquaintance with her and, therefore, anticipated and foreshadowed the tragic events of the following year. She gave António the impression that she was available for love and an extramarital affair. In addition, she also spoke better English than Mr. João Miranda, a tremendous asset for António who wanted to impress his contacts in Boston and New York in the company of a sexy young woman who could pass for his personal secretary. This would have given him a huge power trip, no doubt, one that would satisfy his sense of vanity.

Men from António's generation in São Miguel, men who in the early 1960s were in their early forties, and who enjoyed a certain social standing on account of their work and means, as he definitely did, perceived women in general, single or married, as possible lovers. Given the right circumstances, they would not think twice before engaging in some extramarital love affair. António, after thirteen years of married life, was undergoing a mid-life crisis. He was listless and somewhat bored by his relationship with Elzira. He felt the need to add a bit of spice to his daily life. Elzira's sudden illness, which will be discussed in the next chapter, did not improve matters. Consequently, when he saw how much Laura admired and found him attractive, he was flattered and perceived her availability as an opportunity not to be missed. He encouraged it by flattering her, too. But he also did more than compliment her, he lied to her by not revealing that he had business partners back in São Miguel. He did not want to diminish himself in her eyes. He was on a power trip.

That said, there was a problem that needed to be overcome with time, and the problem was that she was married to Aníbal. How could their relationship flourish under the scrutiny of a jealous old husband? Potential lovers are, however, resourceful people and where there is a will there is a way. They would find a solution to get around this difficulty. And that they did.

Needless to say, António was on a high for the balance of 1960 and the eight months leading to his second trip to the US in August of 1961. He spared no effort preparing for it. He was convinced that if the outcome of the 1960 trip had been good, the one in 1961 was going to be even better, both from business and personal points of view. According to the letter that he sent to his wife dated August 20th, 1961, the last one that he would ever write to her, António states that there was that particular year an incredible demand for fava beans in the eastern coast of the US. Was it being used for personal consumption or to feed horses? For *açorianos*, there are a few delicious dishes whose main ingredient is indeed the fava bean. For *continentais*, as people from mainland Portugal are referred to, on the other hand, they are not much appreciated in any kind of dish and are used mostly to feed animals. Given António's Azorean background, he probably thought that the Americans were interested in the fava beans as a culinary delight. That certainly would be the case for the numerous Azoreans living in America. Irrespective, the eventual fate of the fava beans did not matter. From a business perspective, what really mattered was the fact that American companies wanted to buy this particular product. Also, from a personal point of view, love was in the air. What could go wrong? Fate has a way of undermining sometimes the most careful plans and hands people a surprise.

12

Elzira's Sudden Ilness

Just a few months after the magnificent trip to Continental Portugal and Madeira, Elzira fell ill. Suddenly, she developed a sharp and persistent pain on her right knee that prevented her from walking properly. She felt incapacitated. As the days passed, the situation worsened. A number of physicians were consulted one after the other and none of them seemed to figure out the exact cause of the problem. Finally, someone recommended that she consult a popular physician known in Ponta Delgada as Doutor Alemão (his real name was Dr. M. A. Friedmann) because of his German family background. Germany in Portuguese is translated as *Alemanha*. Being a male, he would be known in Portuguese as *alemão*, which explains why the locals simply called him Doutor Alemão. The fact remains that the good doctor had medical degrees from the University of Leipzig and the University of Lisbon and spoke Portuguese. After taking numerous x-rays of the knee in question, this fellow recommended that a cast be put on her leg going from the foot all the way to just above the knee. The idea was, of course, to immobilize the knee for a period of time to see if the pain would vanish as a result of the immobility. It worked.

It goes without saying that this particular course of action impacted even more severely on Elzira's already compromised freedom of movement and, I am sure, did not do anything for her self-image. She was thirty-six years old and in the prime of her life. Aside from the fact that it must have been difficult carrying the cast's weight around, it was even more depressing seeing herself handicapped in such an obvious manner. So, except for the periodic trips to the doctor, she was essentially housebound for months.

Did the intimate relationship between husband and wife suffer as a direct consequence of her unexpected ailment? It probably did. António, in his postcards and letters from the US, always makes it a point of informing himself about the problem and whether she is feeling any better. He seems to be genuinely concerned about it. That said, Elzira's health trials and tribulations must have had a negative impact on their everyday life as a couple and in their social life too. That would have been inevitable under the new reality.

One is left to wonder whether Elzira's illness was psychosomatic to some extent. Her husband was about to take off to America on a business trip where, inevitably, he would come across Laura, an old rival. So, did she make herself sick in order to play the victim so that António would feel sorry for her? The human brain works in mysterious ways and is capable of bringing about real physical illnesses.

Elzira's predicament lasted for an entire year, until September of 1961. António was already dead and buried when she was freed from the cumbersome cast and put in a position to resume her daily activities without physical constrictions of any kind, and that was a blessing because she had a thousand other problems to face and solve all deriving from his untimely death and her new status as a widow. She was going to have to face an uncertain future alone and she had a young son to raise and protect to make sure that he grew up to become a decent human being. Believe or not, her disease disappeared as if by magic at the same time that a new resolve and purpose in life took hold of her.

As a side note, many years later, in 1976, when we were already living in Toronto, my mother succumbed to another ailment, one that was much more serious than the first one; Dr. Joseph B. Houpt and Dr. Jack M. Coleman, both specialists at Mount Sinai Hospital, in Toronto, diagnosed her with scleroderma, a disease that slowly but surely attacked one by one all the major organs in her body and, if that were not enough, deformed her physically too, especially her hands and fingers. Consequently, she had to give up her modest job in a factory making cosmetic products under the banner of Elizabeth Arden. She, nevertheless, courageously lived with the terrible disease for the next five years and eventually died from it while on a trip to São Miguel in 1981 to attend the wedding of the eldest daughter of one of her cousins, Mr. Eduardo Faria, the same man who had lent her the money for the trip when we emigrated to Canada, and who had attended, together with some members of his family, my own wedding back in the summer of 1978 in Somerville, Massachusetts. Elzira was only fifty-seven years old when she passed away in Ponta Delgada. Dr. Virgílio António de Paz Ferreira, the physician who recommended that she be hospitalized at the Hospital de Ponta Delgada on November 18th, wrote on her death certificate that she died of heart failure. If a defibrillator had been available at the hospital and put to use, she probably would have survived for a while longer. In any case, in spite of her serious illness, Elzira felt that she had to attend that particular wedding out of a very strong sense of duty. For her, it was simply the right thing to do. Curiously enough, both of my parents perished while on trips. Life is indeed full of surprises, twists and turns, and some bizarre coincidences that leave one wondering about the meaning of it all.

13

António's First Trip to Boston and New York

António's first trip to Boston and New York City, in August of 1960, was radically different from the one that followed it in 1961; it was a success story as opposed to a disaster of major proportions. It was also the most important of the two in this regard: it set in motion the wheels of Fate and the tragic event that unfolded in 1961.

During his stay overseas, he wrote four letters to Elzira and, aside from those, he also sent two postcards, one for each one of us. Besides this documentation, there exists as well a few photographs taken either by him or by his friends and acquaintances in different places throughout New England and in New York City.

The 1960 trip marked the first time that António was traveling by airplane anywhere in the world, and it was also the first time that he was going to a foreign country whose language he did not command in spite of having taken private lessons in order to get by when conversing with anglophones. This handicap, however, did not seem to bother him at all because, once in America, he was counting on his friend and business associate, Mr. João Miranda, to serve as an interpreter during his business meetings with representatives of both the Musolino and the L. N. White companies in Boston and New York. Furthermore, he possessed lots of confidence in himself and a sense of adventure which permitted him to look forward to the opportunity with optimism. So, he must have been quite excited about the forthcoming trip itself as well as what he would encounter on the other side of the Atlantic, in a country where so many Azoreans had established themselves and had prospered beyond their wildest expectations. He must have thought to himself that if they had done it, so could he.

The first leg of the trip took him from São Miguel to Santa Maria on August 21st. He took a small propeller airplane, a twin-engine De Havilland, 104 Dove, operated by SATA, an airplane that did the runs between São Miguel and Santa Maria and São Miguel and Terceira on a regular basis and that accommodated a total of nine passengers. Once in Santa Maria, he was scheduled to board a Pan America Airlines (PAA) airplane to Boston. However, when he found out that it was going to be a propeller airplane, most likely a Constellation, an airplane much used by a variety of airliners such as PAA, Air France, KLM, and others to make the transatlantic trip between Europe and the US, or vice-versa, in the 1950s and early 1960s with a refueling stop in Santa Maria, he opted to take one of the early jets from Aerovías Guest, a Mexican company which later, when it declared bankruptcy, was bought by Aeronaves de México. The jet took him to Bermuda, which was really out of the way and not at all in António's initial itinerary, where he spent part of the day before boarding a connecting flight to Boston arriving at Logan International in the evening. He stayed in the US from August 21st until September 10th.

First impressions tend to be important and usually leave lasting memories, especially when one is highly impressionable. António, throughout his stay in the US, seems to have been in a state of total mental alertness, a state of mind that made him super aware of his new surroundings. It was the novelty of it all that left him with indelible memories of the trip. As was his habit, and as the trip unfolded, he took the time to write about his experiences to his wife and me back in São Miguel. And, once he was back in the island from his unforgettable adventure, he would willingly indulge his family, friends or just plain acquaintances, with stories and anecdotes about the "Promised Land" and its people.

14

A Brief Stopover in Bermuda Generates Two Postcards

Upon arriving in Bermuda, António was transferred from the airport to the Castle Harbour Hotel, one of the finest hotels in the island that catered mostly to American tourists with money to spend, in order to freshen up and rest for a few hours before starting the next leg of the trip that would take him to Boston later on that very day. At the hotel, he was assigned room 311. He quickly went up to his room and was most impressed by its level of comfort. Once freshened up, he decided to explore the rest of the hotel and its facilities. The overall luxury of the Castle Harbour and the many amenities that it provided to its guests, such as swimming pools, tennis courts, sailing boats, etc., amazed António. None of the hotels where he and Elzira had stayed in mainland Portugal during the famous 1960 trip compared favorably with it. One of his first stops was at the hotel's gift shop where he bought a couple of postcards: he chose one that showed the hotel itself for me, and then he picked a second one for his wife displaying a lovely Bermudian beach. On them, he wrote a few words explaining how the trip was going so far and, at the same time, describing his first impressions of Bermuda. How typical of him to want to send postcards from different places to keep in touch with his family and to show that he was thinking of us! The few hours that he spent in and around the Castle Harbour were most pleasant and they bode well for what was to come later on. They provided him with a foretaste and an indication of how well the entire trip itself was going to play out before his very eyes. He was going to be exposed to a multitude of new experiences that would definitely enrich him as a human being. He felt privileged, no doubt, as an Azorean, to be able to travel that far in the world. Also, he felt physically good and was in a great frame of mind, one that kept him focused on what he intended to accomplish during the trip.

In his postcard to me, he writes:

Bermuda, 21 Agosto 960,
Meu querido filho. Este é o hotel de onde o pai te está a escrever às 8 horas da manhã, horas daqui, ou sejam 7 horas daí. Espero que te portes muito bem e não consumas tua mãe que como sabes está doente.
Beijos do teu pai.
A. Machado

(Bermuda, August 21st, 960
My dear son. This is the hotel from where your father is writing to you at 8 o'clock in the morning, local hours, that is to say 7 o'clock where you are. I hope that you will behave very well and that you won't make your mother worry because as you know she is sick.
Kisses from your father.
A. Machado)

Aside from the reference to the beautiful hotel, the time difference between Bermuda and the Azores, António zeros in on a very important fact, typical of any caring husband and father: he is hoping that I have been behaving myself because my mother is sick. And he signs off in his usual manner when writing postcards to me. He is sending me kisses. He is a caring father who loves his boy and wants to let him know that he is on his mind.

And, in the postcard to Elzira, he writes:

> *Bermuda, 21 Agosto 960,*
> *Minha Querida,*
> *Depois de uma demora de cerca de 1 hora em Santa Maria, embarquei no avião da Guest e cá cheguei passadas 10 horas de vôo que foi uma maravilha. Saudades e beijos para todos. Melhoras para ti.*
> *A. Machado*
> *Estou a fazer a barba e na minha frente está a andar de um lado para o outro um Zepelim.*

So, António begins in the usual way when addressing his wife, that is to say he refers to her as *Minha querida* (My darling) and, afterwards, he mentions the wait time in Santa Maria before boarding the next airplane and the duration of the flight to Bermuda: ten hours. He states that it was a most pleasant flight. He is sending his love and kisses to everyone, and wishing a quick recovery for her. After signing his name, he makes an interesting observation: he is shaving and, at the same time, he is seeing a Zeppelin going back and forth in front of the room's window. Definitely not the sort of flying object that one would see in São Miguel and, consequently, something of immediate interest to himself and family members back home.

As his short stay in Bermuda drew to an end and as he prepared to return to the airport, António must have thought to himself that things were working out beautifully for him. So far, the two flights had been uneventful and actually rather pleasant. If he had had any apprehensions about flying at all, given that it was a first for him, they seemed to have evaporated totally with the recent experiences. António was feeling rested, relaxed and ready to take the next flight which would take him to Boston's Logan International Airport. He was anticipating an amazing time in America.

15

Four Letters and a Postcard Sent from the US

There are several aspects about António's four letters and three postcards that strike the reader immediately. As everyone knows, when writing a postcard, one has to be notoriously brief and to the point. António's are not an exception to this rule. That said, what makes his postcards unusual is the fact that he includes in them some details that will make the reading interesting and memorable as shown in the previous chapter. The habit of writing postcards is, of course, an old habit of his. During the month-long trip to mainland Portugal, in the spring of 1960, he had sent me a postcard every single day from different places. When writing letters, on the other hand, one has the luxury of space and, therefore, of expanding on the information provided and of expressing one's thoughts and feelings in the process. António's letters provide a wealth of details about what he is seeing and doing. He wants my mother and me back in tiny Ponta Delgada to have a sense of what he is experiencing as his trip unfolds in the New World. It is in his letters that he proves without a doubt that he is a curious and keen observer of people and things, and that he possesses a sense of humor. Finally, he also wants both of us to know that he misses and loves us.

In his first letter, dated August 21st, he starts by giving his wife a detailed description of his immediate surroundings in Bermuda. He notices that there are "rich" American tourists everywhere and that many of them are dressed in shorts irrespective of their age and their physical appearance, a fact that amuses him as in Ponta Delgada nobody in 1960 would dare step outside the home in shorts.

The Castle Harbour had everything imaginable under the sun to make the stay of its guests as comfortable and enjoyable as possible. So, there was a casino, a cinema, several restaurants, ball rooms, a golf course, tennis courts, swimming pools and a plethora of sea activities available to accommodate every aquatic sport. And, so that Elzira has a concrete idea of the high level of luxury that he is talking about, he refers to the hotels where they had stayed during the trip to mainland Portugal by stating that even the best of them could hardly be compared to the Castle Harbour. As for the small Terra Nostra Hotel, one of the finest hotels in São Miguel in 1960, located in Furnas, he claims that by comparison, it is no more than a simple *pensão*, essentially a one-star hotel.

He also marvels at the beauty of the white sandy beaches which contrast so much with the greyness or blackness of the Azorean ones whose origin came about as the direct result of volcanic activity millions of years ago. He is checking everything in and around the hotel with gusto. All the sights and first impressions provide him with a foretaste of things to come once he gets to his final destination, America. A few hours later, after having had the chance to explore the hotel grounds and the surrounding areas, back at the airport, he is also impressed with the number of "big" airplanes (15!) sitting on the tarmac, airplanes that either brought in tourists or that will return them to the US and elsewhere.

At 5:30 p.m. he embarked on the airplane that took him to Boston. The final leg of his trip took three hours. At Logan Airport, in Boston, no one was waiting for him as he had not announced the exact time of his arrival. So, he and a Portuguese immigrant, whom he qualifies as mentally challenged and a very insecure man, a fellow who had boarded the same airplane in Bermuda, begged him not to abandon him and

António, being the helpful kind of man that he was, took it upon himself to arrange for a taxi and explained to the taxi driver that he and the other passenger would be travelling together to Somerville leaving first himself at his friend's place and, afterwards, dropping the other occupant at his own house. António mentions how proud he is of the fact that, in spite of his mediocre knowledge of English, he was able to converse with the taxi driver and make himself understood.

In Somerville, he stayed at an old neighbor's house from Ponta Delgada, Mrs. Maria Lucília Teixeira Rivieccio, Lucília for short who, on September 8th, 1949, had married, in São Miguel, Mr. Joseph Rivieccio, an American of Italian descent living in Boston, and who had emigrated to Boston as a result of her marriage. More recently, she and her children had visited São Miguel during the summer of 1959. However, when António finally got to the house, no one was expecting him there. They were at work. He had not bothered to send Lucília a telegram announcing his imminent arrival. That, however, did not matter because, once finally in their presence, they were delighted to see him. Hugs and kisses followed and before long another friend was alerted of his arrival and joined him and Lucília's family for an evening of reminiscing that lasted until two o'clock in the morning.

The next day, August 22nd, Lucília's husband accompanied him to downtown Boston to see the people at the Musolino Co. Joseph was going to serve as an interpreter. António is extremely focused on what he needs to accomplish in the US. He is there to take care of business and, in the process, create a good impression. First contacts are always critical and, by the time António walked out of the company's office, he was feeling very good about the people who ran the company on account of their professionalism. Once this first meeting was out of the way, António was ready to relax a bit and see some of the local sights.

Every Azorean loves the sea. António was no exception to the rule. So, in the afternoon, Lucília's family took him to see some of the local beaches such as Revere, Nahant and Nantucket. Afterwards, all of them went to visit a common friend. In this first letter, he also mentions that he had already spoken with Laura on the phone and that she and her husband were going to pay him a visit that very evening. António had been in America for less than a day at this stage and he had not wasted any time before letting her know that he was in town. Why? What did he have in mind? Regardless, her eagerness to visit him that very evening at Lucília's home probably pleased him a lot and made him feel good about himself, too.

Everywhere he went, António states that everyone was *satisfeitíssimo*, very happy, to see him. The next few days were marked by visiting other friends and acquaintances or greeting them after they finished their day's work at Lucília's home. Finally, he mentions that he had had already the opportunity to do some other local trips in and around Boston before he was going to set out further afield in New England. At one moment, a friend took him to Charles River, famous all over Boston as the favorite hangout of young, and sometimes not so young, lovers and he makes a comment about it stating that at times the only thing that can be seen sticking out of the parked cars by the margins of the river is four feet. In any case, within just a few days he had a good sense of what Somerville, Cambridge, Somerset and downtown Boston looked like and how people lived their lives in America, especially Azorean immigrants.

In his second and third letters, he elaborates a bit more on what he is seeing and doing as he travels about in the company of friends. He is definitely amazed and astonished by the standard of living in America and the sheer size of everything: cities, highways, hotels, houses, cars, etc. The contrast between what he was used to back in his tiny island of São Miguel and the *fartura*, abundance, displayed everywhere he goes makes him realize just how deprived Azoreans were and continued to be, an impression that he had had the chance to confirm first-hand during his first trip to mainland Portugal. Although the general backwardness of the Azorean people was partially the result of the fact that the Azores is an isolated group of islands in mid-Atlantic with limited natural resources, aside from its natural beauty, to permit and attract development that would bring about much needed jobs to the islands and a thriving economy, there was more to this story than met the eye, as most Azoreans would say to anyone who was willing to listen. The lack of progress could be placed directly at the feet of the central government in Lisbon, a government that neglected for centuries the Azores. So, the reality for the vast majority of Azoreans was that if you happened to be born there, you could not avoid realizing its obvious disadvantages. This isolation is responsible, partially, for the most common dream for Azoreans with imagination, initiative and a sense of adventure: to depart for greener pastures as soon as possible where the sky is the limit. The so-called *insularidade* (insularity), really isolation or remoteness, has always posed a challenge and is one of the most common themes in Azorean literature. Entire generations have left the Azores and established themselves in Continental Portugal, and elsewhere around the world looking for a better future, especially in the US, Canada, France, Brazil and elsewhere.

In New England, António also had a chance to visit many places further afield such as: Taunton, Providence, New Bedford, and Fall River where a lot of the Azorean immigrants established new roots including, in the last one just mentioned, his friend Mr. João Miranda. He stayed at the Mirandas' home for a couple of days and, as a good host, his friend took him sightseeing all the way to touristy Provincetown, a quaint little town at the tip of Cape Cod. To sum up, in the short period of time that António spent in New England, he covered a lot of ground and, consequently, must have drawn some conclusions as to what the countryside and the people who inhabited it were like.

As an aside, it must be said that in some of these New England cities, such as New Bedford and Fall River, there are large communities of Azoreans and, particularly, of people from São Miguel. Given the nature of António's job at Governo Civil, and his friendly, gregarious disposition, António knew quite a few of them whom he mentions by name in his letters. Also, on a business level, it made sense for him to let as many people as possible know that he was into the business of exporting Azorean products. They could be eventual clients. So, in this part of New England, he made the rounds with Mr. João Miranda before returning to Somerville. Furthermore, it had been previously agreed between the two of them that Mr. João Miranda would be accompanying him to New York to serve as an interpreter when it would be time to see the Musolino and White Companies there. And, when that moment came, António fell in love with New York. The only other big cities that could serve as reference points for him were Lisbon, the capital of Portugal, that he had visited with my mother earlier on in 1960 and, most recently, Boston that he had just discovered in the company of his friends and which he describes as a sea of lights at nighttime in one of the letters. But, as he quickly found out, no other city could possibly compare on an equal footing with New York.

In his postcard sent from the Big Apple, he refers to New York as the biggest city in the world. He is amazed by the sheer size of the place, the height of the skyscrapers, the length and width of the roads, the traffic congestion, the number of restaurants and stores, and so many other features. Everywhere he goes he takes his camera, the Agfa Solinette II, to take some pictures to show his family and friends back home, in tiny Ponta Delgada.

António's main objective during his first trip to America was, as I pointed out elsewhere, to meet personally the bosses of the two companies that he had been corresponding with for the last few months in order to put faces to names. It was part and parcel of his business philosophy, that is to say to develop a personal relationship with the people that he was dealing with. It seems that António was impressed by the personnel at the Musolino Co. much more so than with the one from the White Co. Consequently, plans for the next export season, that of 1961, were ironed out and agreed upon between the parties involved. António was delighted with the friendliness and willingness of the Americans to do business with him. He also noticed that Mr. João Miranda was not as fluent in English as he had led to believe. Instead of simplifying main points of discussion during the meetings, he tended to confuse and complicate matters. He made a mental note about his friend's flaw in view of replacing him at some future point with someone else who was more fluent and perhaps smarter, too.

For the time being, however, after completing their business meetings, the two friends were free to go sightseeing and they took full advantage of the opportunity. They visited the Statue of Liberty, The Empire State Building, Central Park, Times Square, Radio City, etc. The trip to New York had been, by all accounts, a success. They were ready to return to Boston or, to be more precise, António to Somerville and Mr. João Miranda to Fall River.

As his trip to America progressed, António must have thought that he had been born in the wrong place on Earth. He kept on observing everything around him with a sense of wonder and bewilderment and had the presence of mind to record his thoughts and feelings as he discovered his new surroundings. His letters give us a measure of the man that he must have been.

His fourth and last letter, dated September 8th, is totally different in tone and content from the previous three. One of the first comments that António makes after addressing his wife in the usual manner is that he is extremely surprised with her lack of news and compares the two letters that she managed to write him to simple postcards due to the lack of content. He is hoping that my mother's short letters were not because she was sick or, for that matter, anybody else in the family.

Then, he goes on to inform her that he had already been to New York in the company of Mr. João Miranda to meet the bosses of the Musolino and White Cos. and that, afterwards, he had stayed at the Miranda's home in Fall River.

Afterwards, he moves on to another topic of the utmost interest, one that will determine his future actions: he says that the previous Monday, September 5th, had been a national holiday in America, it was the Labor Day long weekend, and that the Jesse family, that is to say Laura, Aníbal and Walter had invited him not only for lunch, but also for supper at their home located on Powder House Boulevard, in Somerville.

Throughout the afternoon and the evening of that fateful day many aspects of António's business were discussed and some sort of an arrangement was worked out for Laura to serve as a personal translator of his business letters and, perhaps, even as an interpreter in the future. Aside from António's future business endeavors, it's evident that other conversation topics surfaced such as the ongoing renovations at the Machado family home initiated by him and the bickering and animosity that it was creating among his siblings and himself. Not to mention, of course, another subject that always comes up when *micaelenses* get together anywhere in the world: finding out the latest news about what is happening in Ponta Delgada and the rest of São Miguel.

Let's remember that by the time the Labor Day holiday rolled around, António and Mr. João Miranda had already been to New York and António had had a first-hand chance to determine that his friend's abilities in English left a lot to be desired. By contrast, he was impressed by Laura's command of the language (although judging from the quality of the translations that she provided, it was far from perfect), by her looks, she was thirty-five years old, and by her grasp of the business potential of what he was trying to accomplish. She had much more confidence than Mr. João Miranda, and this would be a definite asset if he were going to impress his business partners in the US going forward.

Further along in the letter, António also states that the very next day, on Tuesday, September 6th, he went to downtown Boston with Lucília to look for some gifts for his family. The following day, he does the same with Laura. At some point, they meet up with her sister Zenaida, who works at the First National Bank, and she joins them for a while on their souvenir expedition in the bank's vicinity.

Next, he stresses the fact that he must return to Fall River one more time to settle his account with Mr. João Miranda and that he is going to take advantage of the trip to see another friend in nearby New Bedford, a certain Mr. Alfredo Costa.

Finally, comes the strangest part of the letter. He seems to be somewhat apprehensive about the return trip to Ponta Delgada by airplane.

He is contemplating the possibility of some tragic aviation disaster and, therefore, he proceeds to tell his wife what she must do if he does not survive it. To that end, he is forwarding two cheques to her. She must keep them until he arrives. However, if he does not make it, she is to cash them and pay very specific amounts to his business partners in São Miguel. All this is explained in detail so that no confusion can result as to who owes money to whom. He concludes by saying the following about his personal finances:

> *... o que restar [do dinheiro do negócio depois dos sócios serem pagos] são teus e do Roberto juntamente com o dinheiro que aí tenho nos Bancos Micaelense e Português do Atlântico, só devendo ser liquidada a letra de 85 contos que tenho no Banco depois do Dinis [Mr. Dinis Mota Soares] pagar a que sou fiador dele ou sejam 50 000$00. [...] Tudo isto para o caso de acontecer algum desastre e não esqueças que tens o seguro também para receber. E, quanto a ti espero que tenhas tido, ainda que não pareça, algumas saudades minhas, Muitos beijos para o Roberto e para ti deste marido e pai que muito vos ama*
> *A. Machado*

(... whatever is left [of the money from the business after the partners were paid of] is yours and Roberto's together with the money that I have there [in Ponta Delgada] in the Banco Micaelense and Banco Português do Atlântico, and the loan of 85 000$00 that I owe the Bank should only be paid off when Dinis [Mr. Dinis Mota Soares] pays his of 50 000$00 that I vouched for him. [...] All this just in case some disaster occurs and do not forget that you still have the insurance to receive. And, with regards to you, I hope that you missed me although it does not seem that way. Many kisses for you and Roberto from this husband and father who loves you deeply.
A. Machado)

The least that can be said about António's feeling of impending disaster and the advice provided to his wife in order for his young family not to be ripped off if he were to perish is that it is weird on the one hand, and quite commendable on the other hand. His last words in that letter also leave no doubt that he loved both both of us dearly. Consequently, he wanted to secure and safeguard our future to the best of his ability in case he vanished from our lives.

It seems that his concern about the forthcoming return trip to Ponta Delgada taught him an important life lesson because, on his second trip to America, he not only left Elzira his explanatory notes about the business and personal finances before he left Ponta Delgada, but he also took the time to discuss briefly some details with her so that she would not be totally in the dark in case he did not return. The moral of the lesson is quite obvious: nobody knows for sure what the future reserves for anybody. There is a Portuguese saying that asserts that *Mais vale prevenir do que remediar* (Prevention is better than the cure). Sound advice, indeed, when it comes to most life experiences, especially those dealing with one's personal finances and the future well-being of loved ones.

16

Rekindling of an Old Flame

Whatever was discussed on that fateful Labor Day holiday weekend at the Jesse residence on Powder House Boulevard, it brought about almost immediate results because as of Wednesday, September 7th, Laura and António went to downtown Boston alone to look for some gifts for his family and friends back home.

Once the shopping expedition got underway, it's not hard to imagine the possible topics of conversation between the two of them. If nothing else, the shopping spree would have been the perfect opportunity to rekindle their old relationship.

So, I suggest that they talked about the good old times in Ponta Delgada when both of them had been much younger and, perhaps, in love, and what eventually had driven them apart resulting in António marrying Elzira and Laura a much older American citizen of Azorean background, Aníbal, who happened to be visiting São Miguel in search of a young bride in the late 1940s. He possessed something that was in high demand for Azorean women of all ages without means: American citizenship. It was a definite asset for a woman in Laura's position, one who had been forsaken by a man whom she admired for all sorts of reasons: not only was António a smart young man with a permanent job in the local government, but he was also good looking and, furthermore, came from a perceived good family, one that she knew very well on account of living in the same neighborhood and being friends with

António's sister, Aida, which meant that she spent a lot of time at the Machado's residence. But, for unknown reasons, their relationship had gone sour. So, when the American came along and proposed marriage to Laura, she did not hesitate long in making up her mind that her future belonged elsewhere. She figured that she had nothing to lose and everything to gain by getting hitched to him, even if that American was an old man compared to her; in 1947, he would have been already in his late fifties and she a mere twenty-one-year-old. Irrespective, she was a woman who was desperate enough to want to escape from a city and an island that offered her no prospects for a decent future. In contrast, for Aníbal she was a good catch. A beautiful young woman, a personal trophy, someone to be displayed and paraded publicly in Somerville. If some gossiper bothered to tell him something about her past, it did not influence his decision to propose marriage right away to the frantic *micaelense*. Besides, chances were that in Somerville nobody would know many details about her background, so he thought. The fact remains that Laura accepted to marry him and, shortly afterwards, was on her way to the "Promised Land".

Next, António and Laura probably discussed at leisure their particular relationship as it stood and made some decision as to what shape it would take going forward. Would they be lovers?

Finally, the topic of António's export business surely came up once again and she most likely offered her services as a translator of his correspondence which, I am sure, he accepted immediately given his mediocre command of English. She would definitely be an asset to him when it came to dealing with the Americans.

That said, one is left to wonder about Aníbal's role in this *ménage à trois* in its early stages of development. He must have sensed that there was some connection, most likely physical attraction, between his young wife and António. Did he accept it as inevitable, as a small price to be paid in order to be married to a thirty-four-year-old woman when he was so much older, almost seventy, or did he resent it and feel hurt and betrayed by the woman that he had saved from misery and brought to America? It's difficult to believe that he would not have harbored some jealousy, if not animosity, towards Laura and, especially, António all the while witnessing the renewed friendship between the two of them blossom rapidly under his very own nose. But, was it enough to sow in his mind the seeds of a plan of sweet revenge that would mature during the rest of 1960 and that would finally come to fruition on the weekend just before August 22nd of 1961? Who is to say what a duped old husband is capable of conceiving, and much less executing, in order to remedy a blow to his sense of honor, dignity and self-esteem? This hypothesis, as I recall, was the one espoused by Virgínio, Elzira's father, a shrewd and cunning man with much life experience on account of his numerous interpersonal contacts as a taxi driver. It was an explanation that made sense to him given his knowledge of what transpired in America in August of 1961.

Aníbal, let's face it, as an ultra-conservative Azorean immigrant born in 1890, someone with a basic level of education, and a strong sense of his prerogatives vis-à-vis his wife, would never have tolerated playing second fiddle in a relationship that involved her. That would not have been the psychological profile of the typical Azorean male of any age group in 1960. His relatives, friends and acquaintances would have perceived him as a *cornudo*, a cuckold, a pejorative term in the Portuguese language used for males whose wives cheated on them. These men would inevitably become a source of public ridicule. Any male of Aníbal's generation who respected himself could not possibly accept being the butt of numerous public jokes about his maleness and lack of sexual prowess. It would have been inconceivable in São Miguel, and unimaginable in the ultraconservative Portuguese communities in the US, for any man to allow to be put in that intolerable and ridiculous situation. And, if that were to happen to him, someone would have to pay a price for his ruined reputation and that person would be António. How to seek retribution remained to be determined. But as the owner of a barber shop in Somerville, I am sure that he came into contact from time to time with all sorts of dubious characters who came in for a haircut or a shave and who were involved in organized crime. Surely some of them would know how to "dispose" of someone efficiently and without leaving behind compromising clues. They would be more than happy to suggest and share with the old barber a few "remedies" to take care of matters if only he were to ask them for some input on the matter.

It is my theory that the mysterious illness that afflicted Aníbal in the spring of 1961 came about when he inadvertently discovered the secret correspondence between his deceitful wife and António. He would have been psychologically devastated by her betrayal, one that caused such mental anguish that it led to depression which, in turn, brought about some form of physical ailment. That said, this hypothesis will remain forever, however, in the realm of pure speculation because there is no evidence to support it or, for that matter, to reject it.

As previously alluded to, it was only in the late 1950s that the idea of going into the export business occurred to António. He was convinced that the superior quality of a variety of products from São Miguel, and a bit of marketing, was all it took for them to be embraced abroad, especially in a country that had accepted countless Azoreans, the US. He only lacked an essential asset as previously mentioned: his knowledge of English left a lot to be desired. So, he needed someone to do the bulk of the speaking for him in America. In 1960, he had relied on his friend, Mr. João Miranda, who had travelled with him to New York. Although António discovered that his friend's command of English was mediocre he, nevertheless, had been capable of making himself understood and the two of them had gotten along famously. Laura, by contrast, spoke better English than Mr. João Miranda and, as an added bonus, had better looks than him. For an aspiring international businessman like António to be seen in the company of a sexy woman, it would definitely have been an added bonus. *Vanité, vanité, tout est vanité*. Vanity, vanity, all is vanity. That being said, there is almost invariably a price to be paid for it sooner or later.

It's fascinating to remark how someone's life can take all sorts of unexpected twists and turns along the way and how Fate eventually catches up with that individual. Who would have thought that António and Laura, so many years after going different ways in their respective life journeys, would be reunited on account of the former's business dealings in the US and that he would die in her arms in a strange hotel room in New York? In spite of many folks thinking that they are in total charge of all aspects of their destiny, good old Fate sometimes has a way of having the last word, after all. Figuratively speaking, Fate put an exclamation mark at the end of António's life.

17

The Secret Correspondence with Laura in 1960-61

In the meantime, unbeknownst to Elzira (individual members of married couples are always the last ones to find out about such matters!) was the fact that António had started corresponding secretly with Laura after his trip to America in the summer of 1960. Essentially, there were two types of letters exchanged between them: business letters, usually asking her to translate his own from Portuguese to English and forward them to the Musolino Co., and more private and intimate ones that he secretly kept locked in one of his desk's drawers at the office at the Governo Civil and that only saw the light of day after his death. The latter were given to Elzira's father instead of to Elzira herself some time before the end of 1961 or early in 1962. An interesting example of how women in general, even a married one and a mother already aged thirty-seven, was disrespected in her person and in her grief by someone at the Governo Civil, someone who certainly had had the opportunity to read the content of those letters when he opened António's desk drawers, and who was intent on embarrassing her in front of her own father. The letters should have been given by this misogynistic character directly to her, not to her father, for heaven's sake!

But, the Ponta Delgada of those days was known as *uma sociedade mesquinha*, in other words, a close-knit society totally dominated by males and where love affairs were a great source of gossip and entertainment for the citizenry. The age of television and soap operas had not yet arrived in São Miguel. So, people entertained themselves by gossiping about each other's lives. Everybody knew about everybody else's affairs. This, of course, is part and parcel of every small-town way of life, even, I daresay, in the Ponta Delgada of nowadays, although to a lesser extent.

With regards to the content of the so-called "intimate letters", one can only speculate about it as none of them were kept by Elzira. One thing is for sure though, they did exist because one of my aunts, another Laura, married to my uncle Francisco, pointed out to me, in one of my trips to São Miguel, that she had read part of one of them surreptitiously and that in it her namesake was saying that she could not stand the fact that António was married to my mother. In other words, she was jealous that Elzira had been the chosen one. Given the circumstances, it is not surprising that my mother destroyed them all to cover up the truth about her husband's illicit relationship with her rival. The destruction of the letters can also be interpreted as an act of protecting her own dignity and self-esteem in her son's eyes. No one likes to be replaced by someone else in a love relationship.

Also, in connection with the confidential letters sent by António to Laura, surely, he would not have been stupid enough to forward them directly to her home address for fear that her husband would discover them. The question that comes up then is, whose address was he using? In other words, who else was in the loop about the personal correspondence between the two of them? One is inclined to believe that the third party involved in this illicit affair was Zenaida, Laura's sister, who lived nearby and who could not only keep a secret, but also keep their compromising correspondence under wraps.

As for the content of the business letters to be translated by Laura, the only extraordinary hint about their renewed relationship is that there is always a little personal note either at the top or at the bottom of the page where António sends greetings to herself, Aníbal and Val. There are no direct clues that something improper was going on between himself and Laura. So, aside from a personal favor on her part to promote to the best of her ability what António was trying to accomplish in the export business in Boston and New York, one cannot suspect her of any ulterior motives. For instance, in one of his last letters to her, dated July 26th, 1961, he writes:

Laura, dentro de alguns dias mandar-te-ei umas amostras de feijão e ervilha. Hás-de fazer o favor de as guardar até à minha chegada. Elas são para mostrar a uns comerciantes de New York, com quem tenho muito interesse em falar pessoalmente e ver se consigo negociar. Como não tenho pressa irão por vapor em vez de avião.
Termino enviando um grande abraço para o Aníbal, Val e para ti os meus mais sinceros agradecimentos. Recebam cumprimentos de minha mulher, do Roberto e de minha mãe.
Abraço-os

(Laura, within a few days I will send you some samples of red kidney beans and peas. Please keep them until I arrive. They are to be shown to some merchants in New York, with whom I am interested to speak in person in order to see if I can negotiate with them. Since there is no hurry, they will go by ship instead of by plane.
I finish by sending Aníbal and Val a big hug and for you my sincere thanks. Please accept greetings from my wife, Roberto and my mother. Hugs.)

There is very nothing in this particular note that would lead one to suspect a love relationship in existence between António and Laura. It's a good example of the so-called "official" correspondence between the two of them. On the other hand, in a rare telegram addressed to Aníbal announcing his eminent arrival in Boston in August, he declares:

Chegarei dia 15 Espero favor ires ou Laura comigo New York Saudades Abraços

António

(I will arrive on the 15th I am counting on you or Laura to go with me to New York Miss you Hugs)

What is most noteworthy about this particular telegram is that António is asking, almost at the last minute, for Aníbal to do him the favor of accompanying him to New York knowing full well that he was going to decline the invitation on account of his job. He also has the temerity to suggest to the husband that if he is not available to accompany him, Laura could go in his stead. One is left to wonder about the husband's reaction upon receiving such a request. By this late date, I am convinced that he knew that something suspicious was indeed going on between his wife and this elegant businessman from Ponta Delgada who was playing the role of a Dom Juan. The man must have been furious when he received such a request.

Let's just imagine, for the sake of the argument, a situation whereby António's friend, Mr. João Miranda, is visiting São Miguel on a business trip and is staying for a few days at the Machados as a guest. Because he has been living in the US for a while, his Portuguese is a bit rusty and he needs someone who is fluent in it to accompany him to a business meeting on the other side of the island, to Ribeira Grande, let us say, the second largest town in São Miguel. He plans to stay there overnight. So, he asks António to accompany him knowing in advance that he won't be able to on account of his job at Governo Civil. Would António at this point propose to him that his wife, who is seven years younger than himself and, therefore, about his friend's age, accompany him in his stead? He would be perceived by other men in his society as a *cornudo* and his wife as a *puta,* a whore. This scenario would be inconceivable in the São Miguel of 1961 and much less in the Azorean diaspora established throughout the world, including the one in Massachusetts that happened to be quite conservative when it came to beliefs, customs and traditions. António would never have allowed this turn of events to develop, and much less to materialize itself, one that would put his own and his wife's reputation at risk. If he were to accept such a proposition, it would be the equivalent of committing social suicide. He would become the laughing stock of all his family, friends and acquaintances. Such a scenario would simply be unthinkable.

So, the question is: why would he put Aníbal in such an untenable situation? The answer is quite simple. António was going through a mid-life crisis at the age of forty-three. He knew that an attractive woman of thirty-five, two years younger than his own wife, was interested in him. He was flattered in his ego that she found him charming, well-spoken, ambitious, apparently with means, and emotionally available. Consequently, António succumbed to the temptation of having a lover before it would be too late in life, irrespective of whether or not he was making her husband look like a fool in the process. By behaving in such a callous manner, though, he was showing moral hypocrisy. He was betraying his own wife, not to mention the trust of a so-called friend. Would there be a price to be paid for his open disregard towards another man's feelings and sense of honor? Perhaps. Was the risk worth taking? Apparently, it was, and he did take it.

As pointed out elsewhere, the second trip to the US was not imperative to begin with. António had already met the previous year his business counterparts there and, therefore, whatever needed to be ironed out between them in 1961 could have been done without his physical presence on the ground. It could just as easily have been dealt with by means of a letter, a telegram or even the occasional telephone call. Therefore, the only logical explanation for it to have taken place is that there was an invisible force that was pulling him there, the allure of a woman who was attracted to him and who made him feel young, alive, and still desirable at the age of forty-three. This last sentence remains in the realm of pure speculation because of the impossibility of knowing for sure what his real motivations were for returning to America since those he took with him to the after-life. Perhaps, after all, he was just following his unique pre-destined life path without unsuspecting it.

António as a dashing young man, 1944; he had begun working for the Posto de Sanidade Vegetal, a branch of the local regional government, on August 17th, 1939, and the position came with a salary that allowed him to enjoy the nicer things in life.

Elzira at the age of 21, December 22nd, 1945; she was a beautiful woman with a sense of flair.

António (third from left) returning from Santa Maria with friends aboard the destroyer Lima, May 2nd, 1947; it was his first time outside of São Miguel and the purpose of the trip was to check out personally the major airport built by the Americans on that island in 1944.

After the wedding of António and Elzira, December 21st, 1947; photograph taken at Foto Nóbrega by Mr. Gilberto Nóbrega; born in Madeira, he had established himself in Ponta Delgada and quickly became the preeminent photographer; the man was an artist.

The wedding party standing on the steps leading to Igreja de São Pedro, the local parish church in Ponta Delgada

A wedding anniversary photograph taken on December 21st, 1950, by Mr. Nóbrega; an annual ritual that lasted until he passed away in 1961

Starting on December 21st, 1952, the wedding anniversary photographs included me!

António in his prime, December 21st, 1955

Elzira in her prime, December 21st, 1955

Virgínio and Margarida Faria, undated; they were Elzira's parents and they were the ones who welcomed their eldest daughter and her son back in their home when she became a widow; it was an arrangement that lasted until December 22nd, 1969, when mother and son emigrated to Canada.

António in his office at the Governo Civil

Part of the Governor's inner circle (António is first on the left)

António (second from left, seated) relaxing with colleagues during an office party

António goes for a swim in the poças, natural swimming pools, of the calhau, rocky shoreline during the summer of 1955. It was a favorite pastime on Sunday afternoons throughout the summer.

The miniscule Dove, SATA's "workhorse", arriving at the Santana Airport, in São Miguel's north coast, December 22nd, 1957; one of the passengers aboard was my uncle José, my father's younger brother, who was returning from Canada; the Dove transported thousands of micaelenses, the inhabitants of São Miguel, to Santa Maria on their way to America or Canada; my father was one of the passengers in 1960 and 1961. In the photograph, my grandfather Virgínio is holding my hand.

Santa Maria Airport, August 24th, 1958; it was, together with Lajes, in the island of Terceira, the main departure-point for Azoreans seeking a better life elsewhere. My father is admiring an Air France aircraft.

The Festivities of Senhor Santo Cristo dos Milagres in Ponta Delgada, São Miguel; it continues to be to this day the major religious festival in the Azores and it attracts thousands from the Azorean diaspora back to Ponta Delgada every year.

Capelinhos volcano off the island of Faial, September 27th, 1957 – October 24th, 1958; the eruption caused a lot of destruction in the western part of Faial which prompted a wave of emigration to America, thanks to the intervention of then-US-Senator, John F. Kennedy.

Cruising in the Azores, October 21st, 1958; the trip included stops in the islands: Terceira, Graciosa, Pico, São Jorge, Faial, Flores and Corvo; it was, for a boy who had just turned six-years-old, an unforgettable experience. António and me aboard the Carvalho Araújo, one of the passenger ships that did the rounds in the Azores.

António loved São Miguel and its beautiful and unspoiled nature. So, either with family members or with colleagues from the Governo Civil who had become close friends, he used to organize many one-day excursions to the island's major points of interest. This photograph was taken at Miradouro da Vista do Rei which overlooks the two lakes and the village of Sete Cidades. It is São Miguel's most emblematic viewpoint.

Mr. João Miranda paid a visit to António in Ponta Delgada on January 8th, 1956. He is second from right; he served as António's interpreter during his first trip to Boston and New York in 1960.

Photograph of the Statue of Our Lady of Fátima. My parents went on an organized trip from São Miguel to Madeira and continental Portugal during April – May, 1960; it was the first and only time that they visited mainland Portugal, and it included a mandatory stop at the religious shrine of Fátima on May 13th; it remained, in my mother's memory, a trip of a lifetime.

At a restaurant in continental Portugal; from left to right: João Bento, my father, Maria Helena, my mother, Mrs. and Mr. Valério, and their daughter.

António, Elzira, Maria Helena, and João Bento walking along the Marginal in Figueira da Foz in May of 1960; a strong friendship developed during the trip between my parents and this older couple and it continued with my mother after my father's demise.

A selection of the 53 postcards, which I collected into an album, from my parents' trip to Madeira and continental Portugal during April–May of 1960; my father made it a point to faithfully send me, his seven-year-old son, who had stayed with his maternal grandparents back in Ponta Delgada, postcards from the different cities and landmarks that the excursionists visited; needless to say, on the back of each one there were brief explanations of the images and even briefer recommendations for me to be a good boy. It's an album that I have treasured throughout my life.

Aníbal and Laura in front of their house in Somerville, Massachusetts, September 5th, 1960; António, the following year, stayed at their house and travelled with Laura twice to New York City. She witnessed him die.

Taken the morning of August 22nd, 1961, in Ponta Delgada, São Miguel, Azores, the day of the tragedy; I am second from left in the front row, and next to me is my cousin, Carlos, who turned six years old that same day.

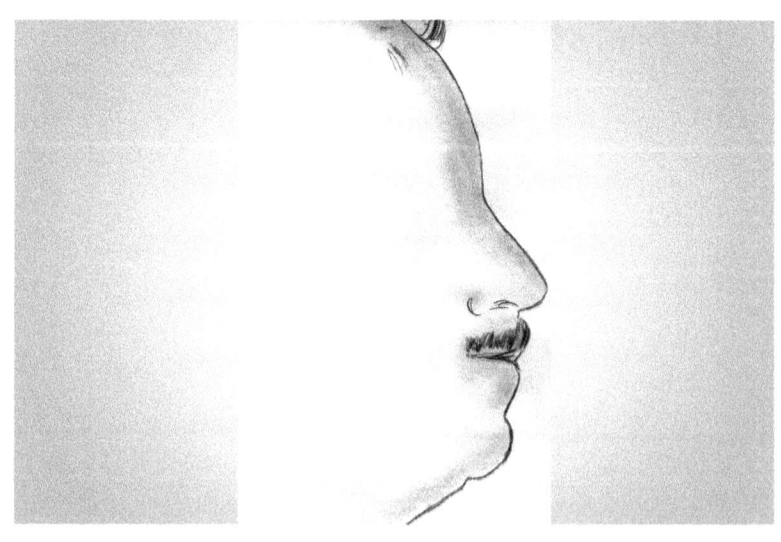

António's caricature as drawn by a colleague, undated.

One of António's favorite personal items at the time of his death in 1961, the Omega Seamaster; over the years he had collected several objects that were dear to his heart; the man had good taste and the financial resources to acquire them.

António's last gift for Elzira: the New York bracelet, August 21st, 1961; it was a piece of jewelry that my mother never wore because it reminded her of where her beloved husband had passed away.

The 8 mm film shot at my father's funeral by a friend of his. A forever reminder of the tragedy for Elzira and Roberto, his wife and son.

TWO

The Tragedy

18

The Fatal Second Trip to Boston and New York

António's second trip to Boston and New York was totally unnecessary from a business point of view. He had already met personally his American counterparts in 1960 and had remained in constant contact with them by regular mail, telegram and, occasionally, by telephone, too. The price of the merchandise had been discussed at length and the final price had been agreed upon by all parties. The method of payment had equally been settled. So, why bother to return to the US within such a short period of time? What really motivated him to want to go there was the secret relationship that he was having with Laura. Nothing else. It was a classic case of fatal attraction between the two of them. Although he did not know it at the time, what was also pulling him to America, in the final analysis, was a date with his own destiny.

António left Ponta Delgada for Boston on Tuesday, August 15th, 1961. It would be the last time that he ever saw his wife and son. He took off from the Santana Airport in São Miguel and, after a short stopover in Santa Maria, he boarded a Pan Am flight to Logan International Airport arriving there at 1:15 p.m. According to the second letter written by Laura to Elzira giving the details of António's passing, he was met at the airport by the Jesse family trio. Nobody else was aware that he would be arriving that day: Mr. João Miranda, his friend from Fall

River, had not been informed about it and, therefore, was nowhere to be seen. Also, the friendly family with whom he had stayed the previous year, the Rivieccios, were not in the loop either. Why so much secrecy? It was deliberate, I suggest, on his part.

The Jesses drove straight from the airport to their home in West Somerville where António was going to be their guest. It's interesting to note that on August 8th António had sent a telegram to them asking for a personal favor; he was requesting that either Aníbal or Laura accompany him to New York to serve as an interpreter. One wonders what effect this unexpected request had on the old barber. Was he surprised by it? Was he counting on António to ask for such a favor? Did he know right then and there that something was going on between his wife and this audacious Azorean? If he did, the man had to be jealous and feel hurt that the woman he had "saved" from a life of poverty back in São Miguel was about to betray him in such a brazen fashion. Did the idea to get rid of the challenger during his stay in the US pop into his head that very day or was it there ever since the Labor Day weekend of 1960? If at this late stage it had not yet occurred to him, he would have a few more days, between the 8th and the 15th, to conceive a plan that would teach the "lovebirds" a lesson that neither one of them would forget any time soon. What would be the nature of his revenge?

In any case, that evening, Laura's sister, Zenaida, came to visit him and the rest of the evening was spent reminiscing about the good old days in the *Ilha*, the Island, that is to say, São Miguel. The next day, on Wednesday, the Jesse family surprised him by visiting an old cousin of his who happened to be in Boston. Afterwards, Aníbal, Laura and António drove to downtown Boston where he met with his local business partners, the Boston branch of the Musolino Co. Then, the three of them dinned in a restaurant, The New Adams House and, afterwards, went to visit Laura's mother and sister returning home later that evening when, while watching TV, António summoned enough courage to ask his host for a most awkward favor.

19

Awkwardly, António Asks Laura's Husband for a Favor

It is at this juncture that the plot thickens, so to speak, because while watching TV António, point blank, asked Aníbal if he could accompany him to New York the following day, that is to say, on Thursday, August 17th, knowing full well that he was going to decline the invitation because it would be a regular working day for him at the barber shop that had been closed for four months in the spring of 1961 due to some unspecified illness of his, one that is only vaguely alluded to in Laura's letters, but one that has been theorized about elsewhere.

One assumes that asking Aníbal personally for this favor must have been, for a decent man like António, a very awkward moment. Did he not feel guilty and ashamed about it? Let's not forget that he was staying as a guest at his home only because the old husband wanted to please his wife for he must have viewed António all along as a rival. But what is really surprising is that Aníbal himself, according to Laura's version of events, upon hearing the request, suggested that she should be the one to accompany António on what was going to be an overnight trip to New York. Furthermore, he seems to have justified his reasoning by stating that Laura was indeed the right person to go with him due to the fact that she was totally familiar with all aspects of António's business dealings with the Americans and, consequently, would be more useful to him than himself who only had superficial knowledge of their details. As pointed out beforehand, she had translated all of his business letters to the American companies and, on occasion, spoken on the telephone with the people in charge.

Aníbal's decision to allow his wife to accompany António to New York is one that is puzzling, to say the least. Was he not aware that there was something special going on between them? Was he not at all jealous? When considering possible answers to these questions, one must keep in mind his age, the fact that he was old-fashioned in his ways and, consequently, would have perceived it as a personal affront his wife running away to New York and staying there overnight with a possible *amante*, a lover. His decision is so much outside of the expected normal behavior for a man of his background and generation that it leaves one utterly perplexed.

Or, on the other hand, was the old man so thankful to his wife for sharing his life that he was willing to accept her unfaithfulness so that she would not be tempted to leave him? Did he consider it a small price to be paid for having married a much younger woman? In any case, as a result of António's unusual request, it was decided that fateful evening that António and Laura would leave for New York the next morning and that Aníbal would drive them to the train station. The "lovebirds" probably did not sleep well that night just thinking about the pleasures that awaited them in the Big Apple. As for Aníbal, what kind of night did he have? He also probably did not sleep well at all. Nevertheless, his reason for not sleeping well was far different from theirs. His insomnia was the result of what was consuming him from within, that is to say sweet revenge. As he lay awake in bed beside his wife, the traitress, did he plan then and there its details? When would it be the best moment to execute it? After the return of the "happy" couple from New York, he probably thought, would be the ideal moment. That would give him a couple of days to figure out the safest and most inconspicuous means to carry out his retaliation, one that would be remembered for a long time.

It is worth pointing out that in the Boston of 1961, right in the middle of raging turf wars between rival Mafia gangs, it would not have been farfetched for the old barber to come into contact periodically with all sorts of shady characters at his barbershop who could have suggested to him several effective ways of eliminating an undesirable rival. Indeed, it would not be farfetched to imagine the possibility that one of his many clients was a mafioso in which case the gangster would have at his fingertips a variety of highly efficient methods of disposing of someone without leaving behind compromising clues. Among the many options available, poison comes to mind. Was it arsenic, the so-called "king of poisons and the poison of kings", strychnine, cyanide or, perhaps, botulinum toxin? Or, was it sodium nitrite, an odorless and tasteless powder that can be easily mixed with coffee, beer or wine? António loved all three beverages and he would never have suspected that someone would have tempered with any one of those drinks. To this very day, occasionally, one still continues to hear of someone being deliberately poisoned when given, for example, a poison-laced drink of some kind. And, through the centuries, jealousy and rage have been potent factors in many crimes of so-called passion. People are blinded by those destructive feelings and act irrationally in order to restore their honor and good name.

20

An Idyllic Round Trip by Train from Boston to New York

So, the morning of Thursday, August 17th arrived and Laura made sure that she was not quite ready for the trip until it was too late to take the morning train to New York and, therefore, to arrive early enough there to take care of António's business that very day. Her plan was facilitated by the fact that one of António's friends, Lucília, in whose house António had stayed in 1960, upon finding out that he was in town, phoned the Jesse residence to say that she was dropping by for a quick visit. Consequently, it was only afterwards that Aníbal drove the couple to the Boston train station. They had with them a couple of *maletas*, overnight bags, containing essentials. As predicted, the afternoon train from Boston only arrived in New York at 5:30, definitely too late to take care of business.

Now, when they found themselves in the train without the annoying presence of Laura's husband watching every move they made, and surrounded by total strangers, they breathed a sigh of relief, I am sure. Finally, they could show openly their affection for one another without fear of being caught and reported. Once seated side by side, Laura took immediately advantage of the opportunity to grab António's hand to hold it tightly in hers. Although there were no witnesses who can corroborate the conversations that ensued between them, one can imagine that some of them went along these lines:

Laura: *António, meu amor, finalmente estamos sós e desembaraçados daquele marido velho e inútil. Temos à nossa frente duas noites só para nós. Vamos poder amar-nos sem medo de sermos descobertos e denunciados.* (António, my love, we are alone at long last and freed from that old and useless husband. We have in front of us two nights just for ourselves. We will be able to enjoy one another without fear of being found out and denounced.)

António: *Sim, Laura. Tens razão. Viver com o teu marido não deve ser nada fácil. Está velho e rabujento.* (Yes, Laura. You are right. To live with your husband must not be easy. He is old and grouchy.)

Laura: *António, querido, não falemos mais nele. Diz-me que me amas, que eu sou e sempre fui a mulher que te convinha.* (António, my love, let's not talk anymore about him. Tell me that you love me, that I was and still am your soul mate.)

António: *Sim, gosto muito de ti. Vamos viver alguns momentos felizes.* (Yes, I like you very much. We will live together some happy moments.)

Laura: *Gostava de te ter só para mim, para sempre.* (I would like to have you just for me, forever.)

António: *Laura, Laura, bem sabes que isso não é possível, nem para ti nem para mim. Tenho mulher e um filho que adoro. Sou responsável pelo futuro de ambos, especialmente pelo futuro do meu filho. O meu pai morreu quando eu tinha apenas treze anos. A sua morte afetou-me para sempre. Tu também és responsável pelo futuro do teu filho. Temos que ter juízo.* (Laura, Laura, you know quite well that that is not possible, neither for you nor for me. I have a wife and a son whom I am crazy about. I am responsible for their future, especially for my son's future. My own father died when I was only thirteen years old. His death affected me for the rest of my life. You are also responsible for your son's future. We have to be wise.)

Laura: *Tens que vir todos os anos a Boston. Não posso viver sem ti.* (You have to come every year to Boston. I cannot live without you.)

António: *Farei o possível para vir.* (I will do my best to come.)
Laura: *Promete-me.* (Promise me.)
António: *Sim, prometo-te.* (Yes, I promise you.)
Laura: *Gostas de estar comigo? Achas-me ainda bonita?* (Do you like my company? Do you still think that I am attractive?)
António: *Sim, gosto. Continuas linda; não mudaste quase nada.* (Yes, I like it. You continue to be beautiful; you have hardly changed.)
Laura: *Que pena não termos casado. Tínhamos sido felizes. Não achas?* (It's a pity that we did not get married. We would have been happy. Don't you think?)
António: *A vida não está nas nossas mãos.* (Life is not in our hands.)
Laura: *É verdade. O destino é cruel.* (It's true. Fate is cruel.)

And, thus, this intimate conversation between Laura and António continued on the way to Grand Central Station in New York. Many other topics of conversation must have come up during a train trip that lasts close to five hours. If nothing else, it would provide the perfect opportunity to bring each other up to date on many and varied subjects. At some point, one can almost bet on it, the conversation turned to more mundane topics such as the ongoing conflict between the Machado siblings caused by António's decision to do renovations in their mother's house and the rift that it had created among them, and Elzira's recent health issues, a topic that would satisfy Laura's sense of curiosity about a rival's health troubles. But however pleasant these conversations might have been, and as the minutes and the hours slowly passed, I suspect that António was becoming acutely aware that by the time that they would reach their final destination it would definitely be too late to accomplish anything of any consequence in connection with his export business. And that, for a man who was intent on finalizing successfully his dealings with both the Musolino and White companies, must have been an unexpected *contretemps* and a source of added frustration and stress, which would explain his increased state of nervousness and the fact that he was chain smoking in an attempt to calm down.

Finally, if those complications were not enough, I suggest that he was already beginning to feel a bit apprehensive and ambivalent about what was going to happen when the two of them would find themselves alone and face to face in a hotel room in New York. In other words, was he about to betray his devoted wife and not feel remorseful about it afterwards? The future would tell. Decisions, decisions. The emotional turmoil that common folks bring voluntarily unto themselves.

21

Pleasure and Business in New York

Inevitably, by the time that the couple arrived in New York, it was too late for them to meet with the New York business partners. The offices of the Musolino and White Cos. were closed for the day. Given that reality, the first priority was to look for a room in a hotel for the next couple of nights. They chose the Abbey Hotel, built in 1927 and demolished in 1982, located on 151 West 51st Street, just East of 7th Avenue, not too far from Grand Central Station. Once in their room, they felt free to take full advantage of the God-given opportunity to engage in intimate relations. However, whether this scenario actually played out or not, we will never know for sure because both protagonists have been long dead and they were the only witnesses of what actually transpired at the hotel. But, let's be reasonable, what else would they have done under such ideal circumstances?

It is noteworthy to remark that in Laura's second letter to Elzira, the one detailing what transpired in New York during António last two days alive, more specifically, with regards to the trip that the couple undertook there on Monday, August 21st, the second one to New York in just a few days, stresses the fact that they were staying in separate rooms. A claim that is contradicted by the hotel bill that shows that only one room was paid for. It's hard to believe that António would have allowed her to pay for her own room given the fact that she was helping him out as an interpreter. He was not only a gentleman, but also a very generous person. So, if that were to be the case, would they have stayed in separate rooms during the first trip to New York on August 17th, too? Most unlikely. Laura, in that same letter, deliberately deceives the widow by avoiding stating the truth which, of course, would have been devastating to Elzira right after António's passing. But the truth has always a way of surfacing sooner or later. And, eventually, it did.

The next day, August 18th, they went to see the Musolino Co. to finalize António's business dealings with them and that was accomplished satisfactorily. Afterwards, the plan was to meet his business partner, Larry White, at the White Co. Regrettably, he was not available and, therefore, nothing could be accomplished. Nevertheless, the secretary told them that she was going to try to contact her boss to see if during that afternoon he would be available to see António. But the much-anticipated phone call from the woman never materialized because, let's face it, it was Friday afternoon and people were already thinking about the weekend, I am sure.

So, the rest of that Friday came and went without any news from the White Co. Consequently, because nothing could be achieved in New York on Saturday and much less on Sunday, the decision was made to return to Boston. That said, Laura is deliberately unclear whether the night of Friday was also spent at the Abbey Hotel or if, instead, the couple returned to Boston that very evening. However, in António's first and only letter to Elzira, dated August 20th, the Sunday right after the trip, he mentions that both of them had returned to Boston the day before which would have meant the Saturday, not the Friday. He would not have mistaken the dates. Besides, as mentioned before, they had waited all afternoon on Friday for the phone call that never came from the White Co., which forced them to miss the last train bound for Boston that evening. Consequently, the inescapable conclusion that one can draw from the information in his letter is that he spent two undisturbed nights at the Abbey Hotel in Laura's company.

One needs to be utterly naïve to think that nothing intimate happened between these two individuals in New York. When Laura offered her services to translate the business letters in the summer of 1960, she was already thinking about the personal advantages that the offer promised to deliver in the future, that is to say the possibility of a love relationship between the two, aside, of course, from some form of financial compensation for the work of translating all the correspondence and serving as interpreter when needed. Given António's magnanimity, there was no way that he would not compensate her for all her troubles. This last point is important because, as far as is known, Laura did not have a job and, therefore, was dependent on her husband for financial support which, practically speaking, meant daily survival.

Curiously enough, nowhere in Laura's correspondence with Elzira can one find an explanation for her not holding a paying job. Her son, by 1961, must have been around eleven or twelve years old and, as a result, old enough to be at home alone while his parents were at work. Her own sister had a job at the National Bank in Boston and, in one of the business letters addressed by António to Laura, there is a reference to the fact that she had just bought a brand-new car and that Laura seemed to be a bit jealous about it prompting António to remind her that to harbor such negative feelings only brought about disappointment and unhappiness. That leads one to conclude that money in the Jesse household was not plentiful given that her husband earned a modest salary as a barber. So, the reason for her not to work for a living remains somewhat of a mystery. In fact, this particular state of affairs was an aberration when compared to what was going on in most other households of Azorean immigrants established in America where the vast majority of wives did work outside of the home in order to help the family acquire all the material goods that it had never possessed in the Azores, especially a house and a car.

My own suspicion is that her husband did not want his much younger wife than himself to be out and about and most likely in contact with other men out of pure selfishness and jealousy. He was protecting his most treasured possession, the woman of his dreams, by isolating her as much as possible from any temptation. But there is more to this opinion of mine because Laura herself seems to have been somewhat pretentious about her social standing within the Azorean community in Somerville and this is reflected in some of the comments that she makes in her letters to Elzira. Although she did not have a lot of education herself, and certainly no professional training of any kind, she felt superior to other fellow immigrant women. She remarks on several occasions that her friends are a cut above the rest, people with so-called "class". Some people are a bit delusional about their self-worth. She seems to have been such a person. By the same token, she also gives the distinct impression of being an unhealthy individual, someone prone to catching easily seasonal ailments such as a cold or the flu and of staying in bed for days in order to recover from them. But more serious than this propensity for falling ill, she comes across as a woman who is always on edge, that is to say the nervous type.

So, with much unexpected free time at his disposal during that Friday afternoon of August 18th, António found time to write a couple of postcards: one to his wife and another one to me. And, in the one destined for me, it's perplexing why he would write that he was not enjoying his stay in New York as much as in the previous year, and that he could not pinpoint exactly the reason for feeling that way. In 1960, on the other hand, he had loved it a lot in the company of his friend João Miranda. Could it have been a case of premonition of imminent disaster? Of having a sense that something awful was about to happen to him and that nothing could be done to prevent it? Of being a pawn at the hands of Fate? Or, alternatively, was he just feeling guilty for having an affair with a woman whose husband he considered a "friend" and for betraying his wife's trust? Why was he experiencing such doomsday feelings? Nobody will ever know for certain what prompted him to write those puzzling final words.

To sum up, in spite of being very busy attending to Laura's desires and his own, António still managed to write those two postcards from

New York to his family back home in Ponta Delgada, something of a tradition for him, which proves that both of us were on his mind. A comforting thought, certainly. And, upon returning to Boston, during the last Sunday of his life, he wrote his first and only letter to his wife, a letter that will be analyzed in detail in one of the next chapters.

22

Unfinished Business in New York

Given that António had been unable to accomplish all he had set out to do in New York on Thursday and Friday, August 17th and 18th, on account of arriving there too late on Thursday to do anything and his business contact, Larry White, at the White Co. being unavailable on Friday, the decision was made to return early Monday morning to the Big Apple to finalize matters once and for all, a decision that was probably made during the return trip to Boston on Saturday morning. That said, convincing Laura's husband of the necessity for a second trip to New York immediately after the first one was a delicate matter. How would they put it to him? I am sure that they thought that the old man would not take it favorably. He would perceive the proposal as another opportunity for his wife to go horsing around with a dashing young man and, in the process, making him look like a fool, a cuckold. Laura, of course, would be the one responsible for convincing him of the absolute necessity of a second trip and, since she was the one in the driver's seat in their relationship, he would accept bitterly her decision as inevitable and final. If he had revenge on his mind, the rest of the Saturday and all of Sunday would be the perfect time to take the bull by the horns.

I have often wondered about Aníbal's reaction to the awkward situation in which he found himself. I mean, the man was seventy and definitely old school and, therefore, jealous of his wife who was only thirty-five years old and obviously smitten by António.

All we know is that by the time that António penned his last letter to Elzira, sometime on Sunday, August 20th, he was complaining of being extremely tired and we also know from Laura's second letter to Elzira that he was complaining of a sore throat that was bothering him and preventing him from breathing properly. Furthermore, to get better, he had asked Laura for a couple of aspirins that Sunday evening. Had he drunk or eaten that weekend something laced with arsenic, strychnine, cyanide or sodium nitrite that would have brought about the symptoms that he was displaying? Who knows?

What is known for sure is that early Monday morning the couple left for New York once again and it was the poor geezer who drove them to the train station. He must have spent an awful weekend just thinking about his predicament.

According to Laura, they arrived in New York in the early afternoon and proceeded to find a room at the Abbey Hotel. To their surprise, no rooms were available because there was a convention going on at the hotel and at the reception desk the couple was told to go to the Paramount Hotel, a sister hotel, located on 46th Street, just around the corner from the Abbey, to book a room there, which they did. And, after a quick lunch, they set out to the White Co. where they were told by the secretary that Larry White was out of the office but that they would get a phone call from him at the Paramount as soon as he returned. So, the two of them returned to the hotel to rest and wait for a phone call that never materialized. As the minutes and the hours slowly passed, António was getting more and more frustrated, nervous and desperate. Things were not going well, certainly not as well as the previous year. Bags of fava beans were unaccounted for in the ports of New York and Ponta Delgada and Larry was nowhere to be found. To keep calm, he was chain-smoking. Also, that particular afternoon was very hot and extremely humid, a situation which aggravated the symptoms that he had started experiencing on Sunday evening, that is to say a sore throat and shortness of breath. He was definitely getting worse by the hour. In short, he found himself unwell and, to further complicate matters, it looked like that they would have to stay at least one more night in New York, something that, clearly, he had not anticipated.

At some point in time and after waiting in vain for the phone call at the Paramount, they decided to go out for dinner and, afterwards, shop for some souvenirs for his family and friends back in São Miguel. That accomplished, they retired early for the night as they were anticipating a busy Tuesday, August 22nd. That night would be António's last one on planet Earth.

It's interesting how one idea leads to another while writing a book. I remember reading, in a travel book by David Sayers about the Azores some years ago, an interesting short article by a doctor named Jane Wilson-Howard about clots and deep vein thrombosis (DVT) associated with long-haul flights, especially those lasting more than 5½ hours, as was António's from Santa Maria to Boston in 1961, that can lead to pulmonary embolus (PE), which is caused by a clot travelling all the way to the lungs and lodging itself there. If this happens, it can be a serious health risk if not addressed right away. In any case, according to the doctor, some individuals are more predisposed than others to DVT among whom are those who are over 40 years old and heavy smokers. To prevent such disasters, she recommends that passengers drink plenty of water or juices to stay hydrated and that they get up and walk around instead of staying immobile for the entire trip. In addition, she emphasizes that they should avoid drinking coffee, alcohol and smoking (the last one was very common during the 1960s), during the flight. Besides these practical suggestions, she implies that another contributing factor for bringing about DVT is the reduced oxygen in cabin air. Finally, she states that usually the symptoms show up three to ten days after a long flight. When I read Dr. Wilson-Howard's description of DVT for the first time and the kind of people that it seems to affect, I was struck by the fact that António was not only over 40, he was 43 in 1961, a heavy smoker, a coffee and alcohol drinker, but also the type of person who did not exercise regularly. Aside from these so-called matches, what struck me the most was the fact that he started complaining about the sore throat and the shortness of breath within the time frame that the good doctor mentions, three to ten days after a long-haul trip. I have wondered ever since if PE also contributed to António's rapid demise.

As everyone knows, determining the exact cause of someone's death is a complicated matter, especially one that occurred a long time ago when autopsies were not as scientific as they are nowadays. In any case, the coroner who performed António's autopsy in New York did not mention pulmonary embolus as a possible cause of death and, instead, established that it had been edema of the larynx without singling out, lamentably, what may have caused it.

23

Two Postcards and a Letter Sent from Heaven

By the time the two postcards and the last letter arrived in Ponta Delgada, António had already died. Hence the title given to this chapter. Receiving them was like getting personal messages from the other world. They not only generated a sense of unreality surrounding his demise but also, concurrently, provided a glimpse as to what his last days alive had been like. Needless to say, their content was thoroughly poured over during the days, months and years that followed the tragic events of the summer of 1961.

As pointed out in the previous chapter, António wrote two postcards from New York on Friday, August 18th. Both postcards show a picture of the Abbey Hotel where he was staying with Laura. On the one to me, he declares that for whatever reason he is not enjoying his stay in New York this time around as much as the last time, and that he cannot pinpoint the exact reason for feeling that way. Aside from this unusual comment, he expresses the hope that I have been behaving myself and that I have not been exhausting my mother who happened to be sick. Here is a transcription of the text:

18 Agosto 61
Meu querido Filho,

Espero que te tenhas portado bem e que não tenhas consumido tua mãe. O ano passado gostei muito desta cidade, este ano não e não sei porquê. Recebe muitos beijos e a benção do teu pai e amigo.
A. Machado

(August 18th, 61
My dear Son,
I hope that you have behaved yourself and that you have not made your mother worry. Last year I liked this city very much, this year not so much and I don't know why not. I am sending you many kisses and the blessing of your father and friend.
A. Machado)

On the postcard to Elzira, he does not start writing in his usual way which would be *Minha querida*, but rather just by writing *Elzira*. The rest of it is rather trivial. He mentions that he has not had the opportunity to see many of his friends and acquaintances, except for one, a former neighbor of his in Ponta Delgada, Lucília, at whose house he had stayed the previous year, but hopes to be able to see them all after returning from New York. This, of course, is all true and it is also an admission that he had not seen Mr. João Miranda whom he claims in his letter of August 20th accompanied him and Laura on the trips to New York on both occasions. Below, I provide its transcription:

18 Aug 961
Elzira; Cá estou, mais uma vez, nesta cidade montruosa, e neste belo hotel, desde ontem. Falei com a Lucília e Família já mas a maoir parte das pessoas conhecidas ainda não as vi. Há-de ser depois de sair desta cidade. Saudades.
A. Machado

(August 18th, 961

Elzira; Here I am, again, in this monstruous city. And in this beautiful hotel, since yesterday. I already spoke with Lucília and Family but most of the acquaintances I have not seen yet. It will be after leaving this city. Miss you.

A. Machado)

In that same letter, the first thing that he says to his wife is that he hopes that she is feeling well. The very next item that he mentions is that he is feeling tired, extremely tired, because of the fava beans. He reports that the ship Açores, docked at the port of New York, has not yet unloaded all the bags containing the merchandise and that, therefore, he does not know whether the bags that were missing from the bill of lading were loaded in Ponta Delgada or not. He is concerned about that eventuality. Afterwards, he mentions the name of his friend Mr. João Miranda twice in different contexts. Firstly, he says that despite João Miranda's best intentions, he is complicating António's life because of his lack of English skills and, secondly, he declares that his friend is expecting to be compensated for his help by getting a commission. This double reference to Mr. João Miranda is puzzling because he did not accompany António and Laura to New York at all. In fact, his friend did not even know that António was in America. However, by mentioning his friend's name twice, one is forced to draw the conclusion that it was deliberate on António's part. He was covering up the fact that he had been alone with Laura in New York, something that would have been totally unacceptable and regarded as a personal affront by Elzira. Next, he deals with some business details; he wants her to contact one of his partners in Ponta Delgada in order for some samples of Azorean products to be sent to him as soon as possible.

Then, he moves on to another hot topic making the news in 1961. He mentions seeing many soldiers and sailors wherever he goes in New York. He refers to the tense situation going on in Berlin. He is alluding, of course, to the Berlin Crisis that had started on June 4th, when the former USSR, through Nikita Khrushchev, the Secretary of the

Communist Party, ordered the Berlin Wall to be built separating East Berlin from West Berlin and creating in the process one of the gravest incidents of the Cold War. Indeed, President Kennedy and Khrushchev brought the world to the brink of a nuclear war that year and António, like many other reasonable and well-informed people at the time, was concerned about the situation because the conflict in Europe had escalated rapidly after the American Bay of Pigs fiasco in Cuba on April 17th. António had lived, after all, through the darkest period of the Second World War as a young man. Consequently, he had good reasons to be worried and to fear for the safety of his family and, especially, that of his young son. Another World War would be disastrous to everyone.

Finally, he addresses Elzira's ongoing illness. He finishes the letter by asking a flurry of questions:

Agora, minha querida, dize-me como tens passado? O Roberto está bem?... Ele tem brincado muito? Tem sido bem ensinado? Foste ao médico? Que te disse ele? Escreve-me para que fique descansado. Muitos e muitos beijos para ambos e cumprimentos para todos. Saudades.

(Now, my darling, tell me how you have been? Is Roberto well?... Has he played a lot? Has he been a good boy? Did you go to the doctor? What did he say? Write to me so that I can relax. Many kisses for both of you and greetings for everybody. Miss you.)

To sum up, his last letter leaves no doubt in the reader's mind that he cared deeply about Elzira and me. Its poignancy derives from the fact that it was written only a couple of days before he died. That being said, he also lies openly in it to forestall any suspicions about what was really going on in the US.

António had left Ponta Delgada on Tuesday, August 15th, in perfect health and full of vitality, enthusiasm and optimism. A mere five days later he states that he is extremely tired and feeling unwell. And, according to Laura's second letter, that very Sunday evening he starts complaining of a *dor de garganta*, a sore throat, which is bothering him. Could this be the early symptoms of some kind of poisoning at work? One wonders. At any rate, if Aníbal was going to do something about the untenable situation in which he found himself, this specific weekend was the moment to take decisive action. He would have most of Saturday, August 19th, and the following day, Sunday, August 20th, at his disposal to implement whatever scheme he had in mind. It is within the realm of possibilities that when he found out that the couple planned to return once again to New York on Monday morning, he decided to carry out his plan. It must have been intolerable for him to see how happy Laura and António were at his own expense and not want to do something about it. He would have his sweet revenge! What form it took is something that family members and some acquaintants familiar with his sudden demise speculated about it for many years.

Jealousy (and a blow to one's ego) leads many times to hate and the feeling of hate is a powerful drug capable of distorting one's moral compass which may, in turn, guide one to harm a human life for the sake of teaching that person an unforgettable lesson. In short, if the old husband was intent on taking revenge, it was then or never for him to take some action. In other words, the moment of truth was upon him.

In any event, as I stated before, on Sunday evening, August 20th, António accepted a couple of aspirins from Laura and seemed to get some relief for his sore throat. Early the next morning, that of Monday, August 21st, he complained once again about the same symptoms. Aníbal went so far as to suggest that António see a doctor before returning to New York, but António laughed at the idea saying that Americans ran to the doctor at the very first sign of any ailment. Was he too proud to admit that he was in fact getting sicker by the hour and in desperate need to see a doctor? It's a definite possibility.

After breakfast, Aníbal drove the couple to the Boston train station. They took the 8:00 o'clock train arriving in New York at 1:30 in the afternoon. Staying at the Abbey Hotel was impossible because it was fully booked for a convention and so they checked in at the nearby

Paramount Hotel. After lunch, they pay a visit to the White Co. where they found out that there were complications due to misunderstandings regarding the overall price to be paid for the merchandise and the terms of payment as well as the rate of commission to be given to the Americans. The meetings took longer than expected which meant that nothing else could be accomplished that day. So, they returned to the Paramount Hotel to rest. António stretched out on top of the bed and, after a while, suggested that they go out for dinner. During the meal, Laura noticed that António was not eating well. Otherwise, he looked fine. After dinner, they decided to look for souvenirs which they did until bedtime. They retired early because the next day, Tuesday, August 22nd, was going to be entirely devoted to concluding business. They would have to return to the White Co. and, afterwards, go to the customs office located in the port of New York to figure out what had happened to some of the bags of merchandise that seemed to have vanished into thin air.

When I read Laura's second letter for the first time, I was struck by her sense of foreboding about António's future. She categorically states that during that Monday evening she had the distinct feeling that he was going to be sick in spite of not having a fever and looking just fine.

As I mentioned in a previous chapter, that Monday had been an exceedingly hot and humid day in New York and the two of them were exhausted by all the running around that they had done without much being accomplished. Let's also keep in mind that António at forty-three continued to be a heavy smoker and that the night before he had complained of a sore throat for which he had been given a couple of aspirins that, apparently, had provided some relief from the annoying symptoms.

Did António's condition deteriorate considerably overnight? It seems to have been the case because, as Laura describes, at 6:15 in the morning of that ill-fated Tuesday, he knocked at her room door, barefooted and disheveled, desperately asking for more aspirins which she promptly gave him. He ran to the washroom to get a glass of water and was able to swallow the first one but the second one did not go down his throat. He was so distressed and confused at this stage that he even forgot that he was supposed to chew the aspirins, not swallow them. However, he was still able to speak coherently and managed to tell her to call a doctor right away because he felt very sick. Then, according to her account, he returned to his room while she called the reception desk to request a doctor for the unexpected emergency. A few minutes later, concerned about leaving him alone in his room, she, in turn, exited her room to go to his. She was stunned to find him standing in the corridor unable to get into his own room. He told her that he could not enter it because he had left inadvertently his key inside when he had gone to her room to ask for the aspirins. At this juncture, she convinces him to return to her own room. Apparently, he hesitates because she is only wearing pajamas. Where did these come from? She says elsewhere that when they had left Boston the day before they expected to return the same day. So, any luggage would have been unnecessary. As for António, we know that he had brought along a *maleta*, a briefcase, which contained his business notes. We know about the *maleta* because of the existence of an official report from the Portuguese Consulate in New York that lists all of António's possessions, one that was based on the official police report. In any case, after some persuasion on her part, he accepts to go into her room. He is definitely unwell. He sits on the edge of her bed and cannot breathe. He is gasping for air. At one moment, he grabs Laura's hand and tries to tell her something important, surely a last thought for his wife or, perhaps, his son, or to tell her to cover up to the best of her ability the affair, but he is already unable to express himself. He begins to lose consciousness and is about to fall to the side. She manages to catch him in her arms and holds him while he slowly dies. That's when she starts screaming for help. Within seconds the corridor is full of stunned guests who are curious to find out what the commotion is all about and, a few moments later, by hotel employees who are followed by the arrival of some police officers. It is pandemonium at the Paramount Hotel. And, according to the only witness, Laura, that's how António exited this world.

24

In the Throes of Death

I have often thought about a person's last reflections in the agony of death. Many authors have pondered this question, a question that will forever remain without an adequate answer for the people most concerned, the dead, never come back to recount their last thoughts and feelings to anybody. That said, the good news is that any individual with a bit of imagination can delve into the subject without fear of being right or wrong about it. Nobody, authors least of all, possess the ultimate answer about such things. Does, for instance, in those last few seconds of consciousness, one take stoke of one's life and the relationships that did matter and what is going to happen to the loved ones left behind? Or, on the other hand, does one focus on what may happen on the afterlife? Did António know with absolute certainty that he would never make it out alive of that room at the Paramount Hotel in New York and see once again his wife and son? And if so, what went through his mind? Was he distraught with panic knowing that they would be left vulnerable without him to protect them? Selfishly, I would like to think that his last thoughts were directed at both Elzira and me but I, like everybody else, will never know for sure. It is fascinating, however, to speculate about such matters knowing full well that the chances of whatever one imagines coinciding with what the particular individual experienced in the throes of death is nothing short of remote. In other words, one is totally free to speculate about such matters knowing in advance that the deceased won't return to point out what actually went on in his or her mind when the big moment finally came.

So, given that this realm is a free for all, I will advance that António's last thoughts were directed at his loyal wife and dear son. He cared for Elzira and thought that the beautiful baby that she had gifted him with was special. They had been married for nearly five years before I had come along and now, at the age of nine, it was as if I had been there all along. The truth of the matter was that my presence had enriched his life and he wanted to be there to guide me as I became a teenager and, eventually, a young man. He remembered how he had felt himself when his father had died unexpectedly in 1930, when he was only thirteen years old, and how his daily life had changed dramatically as a result of the tragedy. As he realized what was happening to him, that his death was not only inevitable, but also imminent, I am sure that he was distressed at the thought that his own son was going to be an orphan, just like he had been one himself. If only he could somehow be saved and return home. But he happened to be in the US, a country whose language he did not master, staying in a strange city, New York, and in a strange hotel, the Paramount Hotel, in the company of a woman, Laura, who was not his wife, a fact that he had deliberately concealed from Elzira in his last letter to her. It must have crossed his mind that the truth, should he not survive, would eventually come to light. If that were so, he would be caught in a compromising situation. Did he feel guilty about it? Did he have regrets? Regarding his wife, he must have realized that she was ill-equipped to deal with any of the fallout from his death. He knew that she had a basic education and that she was only superficially familiar with his business and that, furthermore, she did not possess the confidence to bring the venture to a successful conclusion.

Similarly, he must have known that the family situation at the Machado residence was far from ideal with all the sibling rivalry that had recently surfaced on account of the renovations that he had undertaken to upgrade the house. Perhaps he took some comfort and consolation in the fact that he had put aside some savings and that there was a couple of life insurance policies that would cushion the blow of his disappearance for the two of us.

But who is to say what really went through his mind as he lost consciousness and his heart stopped beating in the arms of a woman who was paralyzed by fear and, therefore, incapable of taking decisive action? A woman unable to react quickly enough to what was unfolding before her very eyes and place an urgent phone call to the concierge at the front desk of the Paramount Hotel explaining the seriousness of the situation. And when she finally reacted by screaming for help and people did arrive, António was already dead.

What puzzles me the most about his death is that as he was beginning to feel worse and worse by the minute, why did he not take the initiative himself of going downstairs to the hotel's front desk to get the prompt help that he so desperately needed? He knew enough English to make himself understood. In addition, given his personality and *savoir-faire*, that's what one would have expected of him because he had been, after all, a problem solver all of his adult life. Could it be that he panicked and got so confused that he froze unable to think rationally? Or, was he just paralyzed by fear of what might happen to him? So many questions left unanswered. I only hope that he did not suffer much in his moment of agony for he had been a good husband and a loving and caring father.

25

A Woman in Distress

Being present at someone's final moments is not a pleasant experience for the vast majority of people. And, if that person is someone that one loves dearly, it's even worse. Laura must have freaked out when she realized what was happening to António and that she would be the only live witness of the occurrence. She was caught in an awful situation. She was in a strange hotel room in New York, a city that she hardly knew, with a dead man in her arms who was not her husband. She must have thought right then and there that she was going to be suspected of foul play by the police and also by the family of the deceased. As described before, her first reaction was to panic, which was followed by screaming for help. Meanwhile, not being able to hang on to António any longer because of his weight, she let him fall backwards on the bed.

On account of António's age, he was only forty-three years old, and because he was a Portuguese bureaucrat and, finally, because he had died in a hotel room in the arms of someone who was not legally his wife, an autopsy had to be performed before the body could be released for burial. So, for the time being, nobody could remove the cadaver from the Paramount Hotel until a pathologist from the city of New York made his death official. In addition, when the police officers discovered that he was a Portuguese civil servant, the Portuguese Consulate in New York had to be informed of his untimely death. Henceforth, its involvement in this tragic affair would be of paramount importance with respect to the release of the body for burial.

In the middle of this chaotic scene, Laura found the presence of mind to call her husband in Boston and tell him what had happened. Apparently, he offered to fly to New York and help out with the aftermath of the catastrophe, but the offer was turned down by her. One would think that she would want her husband to be by her side for moral support in such an awkward situation. But what is really intriguing is that after telling him that António was dead, she told her husband to contact immediately a certain Mr. Costa at the Joseph A. Costa Sons Memorial Funeral Home, a good friend of the family, to make preparations for the funeral. Why such urgency? Laura did not have the authority to make such a decision since she was not António's wife and, besides, she had been told by the police that the coroner's office would be involved in the matter and that an autopsy would have to be performed to determine the possible cause of his death before the body could be released for burial. In addition, it was Elzira's prerogative as his legal wife, not hers, to determine what to do with his remains. That said, in the middle of the ongoing chaos at the Paramount Hotel, Laura also displayed the presence of mind to make sure that António's belongings were properly recorded by the police officer in charge of the situation at hand so that they would not be misplaced at the police station or, perhaps, even stolen by some dishonest hotel employee. It's nothing short of amazing how calm and collected she seems to have been in spite of the dreadful event that she had just witnessed.

In any case, time was moving at a snail's pace for Laura. Eventually, a pathologist from the city arrived at about noon and made António's death official. Ambulance attendants were to pick up the body shortly afterwards to transport it to the morgue for the autopsy to be performed. If someone from the New York Police Department (NYPD) or from the Paramount Hotel kept her company before the arrival of the doctor, it's not known. What is known, nevertheless, is that at some point in time an individual from the White Co. finally phoned Laura's room and, when she told him about António's tragic end, this man quickly made it to the hotel in order to lend a hand to an obvious woman in distress. Once there, he suggested that they go immediately to the Portuguese Consulate to report his death and to ask for whatever help the chancellery could offer. This they did. It was the logical thing to do. It was also something that had already been pointed out to her by the police.

At the Portuguese Consulate, Laura explained that António had passed away at the Paramount Hotel and that he was a Portuguese civil servant. She wanted the Consul to send a telegram to the Governor in Ponta Delgada announcing the sad news so that António's family would be informed through the latter. Also, she expected the Consulate to intervene with the State of New York for the corpse to be released from the morgue after the autopsy had been completed in order for it to be transported to Boston for burial there.

However, given the fact that she was not his wife, she was told that this could not be done without a Power of Attorney from António's widow giving her authorization to deal with the corpse. This document was of the utmost importance and it had to arrive at the Consulate in New York from Ponta Delgada promptly otherwise the body would be kept at the city morgue for the next six months. Upon hearing this news, Laura broke down in frustration and wept openly begging the officials at the Consulate to do something, anything, to solve the impasse and the looming bureaucratic nightmare that all of them were beginning to anticipate.

For the time being, though, since nothing else could be accomplished in New York by her, she was advised to return to Boston and wait for the Power of Attorney to arrive from Ponta Delgada. Once the document received, she was to alert the Consulate right away so that the necessary legal steps could be taken to get the body released from the city morgue and put on a cargo train to Boston if that was what the widow wished. She was told that it was then and only then, with the Power of Attorney on hand, that the Portuguese Consulate could intervene in the matter.

Before leaving the Consulate, still, one more thing needed to be done; one of the officials asked her to make a deposition regarding António's personal objects which she had seen being taken from the hotel room by the NYPD. Unexpectedly, although under tremendous stress, she remembered vividly every single one of them and a list was quickly drawn up. Right afterwards, in her presence, the official made a phone call to the police in order to ascertain the accuracy of the list. The two lists matched perfectly. Given the fact that António had in his possession expensive personal items as well as money, it is surprising that nothing went missing, especially the Omega Seamaster wristwatch which, obviously, in and of itself alone was worth a small fortune. To their credit, the cops who had shown up at the Paramount Hotel proved to be most honest.

So, at long last, Laura was free to return home. The gentleman from the White Co. who had taken her to the Consulate and had stayed with her throughout the deposition, took her to Central Station where she boarded a train back to Boston. She was on her way home with lots of spare time to mull over the unbelievable event that she had witnessed on that Tuesday morning. Obviously, the return trip from New York to Boston was quite different from the one going there. For one thing, she was travelling alone but, as a constant reminder of António's absence now, she was carrying his briefcase with all the notes concerning the fava bean business. It had been quite a day, one that she would remember for the rest of her life.

At some point during the trip, Laura must have thought about how to break the news to Elzira who, in turn, would eventually tell me that I would never see my father again. As a mother herself, she must have felt sorry for both of us, especially for the boy who had just lost his father at such a young age. How would she be able to explain to Elzira that António and her had been alone in New York? How would she answer the thousands of questions that would surely surface concerning his untimely death and the circumstances surrounding it? How would she manage to convince the widow that nothing illegitimate was going on between herself and António when he had died in her arms and in her hotel room? There was a lot to think about. The immediate future did not look at all pleasant for her. She would have a lot of serious explaining to do to all concerned, especially his family in Ponta Delgada

She arrived in Boston at 8:30 in the evening. She was by then a nervous wreck, physically and emotionally drained by all accounts. She was met at the train station by her husband, her sister and a few close friends. Upon seeing Laura's appearance, she looked awful, everybody felt sad for her and for what had happened to António. According to her description of the arrival, they all wept openly, including Aníbal. But, the saddest of them all was definitely her who was living wide awake the worst nightmare of her life, one that would continue for quite some time as the next few days, weeks and months slowly passed.

In the immediate future, the only thing that Laura could do was wait for the Power of Attorney to arrive from Ponta Delgada. Truth be told, the wait time for the arrival of that precious document must have literally killed her. Being the nervous type that she happened to be, and after all the stress that she had undergone ever since the early morning of August 22nd, she was, for all intents and purposes, on the verge of a true nervous breakdown. A couple of days later, to her relief, the Power of Attorney arrived giving her the authority to deal with António's burial as well as his unfinished business with the two American companies. She cried and laughed at the same time with relief to the great astonishment of those present including, unexpectedly, that of the representative of the Joseph A. Costa Sons Memorial Funeral Home who happened to be visiting the Jesses at the time and who had been contacted by the old barber right after receiving news from his wife regarding António's death. As pointed out before, he was not only friends with the Jesses, but he was also now going to be the one in charge of António's funeral arrangements. According to Laura, the Jesse couple had given him lots of business in the past, something that solidified their friendship, I am sure. That being said, to Elzira and Virgínio, her father, who read and reread each one of Laura's letters numerous times looking for tidbits of information to shed light on the possible cause of António's death, his coincidental presence at the Jesse's home looked odd, if not outright suspicious. But then again, they did not socialize with any mortician in Ponta Delgada. As the years came and went, they forgot about the Jesses' particular friendship with him to focus exclusively on the possible role of the couple in António's death.

For his part, but unknown to Laura at this stage, although he had not received the Power of Attorney yet, the Portuguese Consul in New York had already managed to pull some diplomatic strings of his own with New York City officials and had succeeded in getting the body released from the morgue out of respect for a Portuguese civil servant who had passed away in a foreign country. So, when Laura did phone the Consulate to say that she had received the document from Elzira, she was told the good news and was directed to contact a funeral agency in Boston for the body to be transported to that city and the final funeral arrangements to be made. This piece of advice was totally unnecessary since Aníbal had already taken care of the matter.

In short, to the family of the deceased back in Ponta Delgada, especially his widow and close family members, it seemed that everybody was in a rush to bury António's ashes as quickly as possible. Nevertheless, by acting in such a hurried fashion, they raised the level of suspicion in their minds that foul play had occurred although none of them could prove it. All of them were still in the process of coming to terms with the fact that António had disappeared forever from their lives.

26

Barely, Elzira Copes with Tragedy

The night of August 22nd, 1961, must have been a dreadful one for Elzira. I am sure that it was nothing short of a true living nightmare. Her husband was dead and, even worse for her, he had left his business affairs unfinished and in disarray in a foreign country. She was just thirty-seven years old and knew next to nothing about his business. So, possessing limited knowledge about it, and given her basic education and weak personality, she must have realized immediately that going forward would be an awful period in her life. The easy lifestyle that she had become accustomed to for the last fourteen years was about to evaporate into thin air and, what was even more worrisome for her, she had been left with a nine-year-old son.

And, to further complicate matters, she was living in her mother in-law's house where she had never been appreciated and much less welcomed. Right after António's death, family fights became a way of life, especially because he had taken the initiative of renovating the main washroom in the family home and there were bills left unpaid that none of his siblings was interested in assuming as part of their financial responsibility and obligation. Apparently, even though all the people who lived in the house were going to benefit from and enjoy the renovations undertaken, nobody wanted to share in the expenses. Money was tight.

Therefore, it did not take long for the home atmosphere to turn sour and, consequently, Elzira was shown the door in early September of 1961. At her father's suggestion, the two of us moved to his house, located at Rua da Pranchinha, just a short walk to the east of the Machados' residence, where the old bully continued to reign supreme over his wife. Now, as when Elzira was single, he was in a position of power vis-à-vis his daughter once again and never wasted an opportunity to let her know that he was doing her an enormous favor by letting her live in his abode for next to nothing.

As for me, while my father had been alive, my grandfather had treated me kindly and respectfully, but now that he was dead, he showed his true colors and, at every chance, interfered arbitrarily in my life to prove the point that he was the one in charge of everyday routines in the household. It gave him pleasure to be in a position of power to decide whether I was allowed to do this or that, mostly unimportant stuff, just because I was living in his house. The first collateral victim of Virgínio's oppressive behavior was my dog, Bobby. The old man simply refused to allow me to bring the dog along. A cruel thing to do to any child. I was forced, every time I wanted to see and play with my four-legged "friend", to return to the house where I was born and from where my mother and I had been kicked out. An awkward and totally unnecessary situation. This kind of conduct from an adult towards any child is, of course, the trademark sign of a bully.

In any case, my grandfather's behavior was in such a sharp contrast to the way that I had been treated by him in the spring of 1960, when my parents had gone on a month-long trip to mainland Portugal and I had stayed at his house, that I was left utterly confused and lost at first, for I did not understand why I was being treated differently now. What I ignored at the time was that my father had paid his father-in-law a handsome sum of money for my upkeep during that month in 1960. How life had changed for me in the space of just one year! Luckily, my grandmother Margarida continued to be the kind woman that she had always been and did everything in her power to blunt the emotional blows delivered periodically by her husband on all those around him.

Deep down Virgínio was a very frustrated man. His frustration came from three sources: first of all, although he owned his own taxi, which was the latest model at one point but, as time passed, he did not keep pace with the changes in car manufacturing and, before long, he was driving the oldest taxi in town. While other taxi drivers not only had purchased the latest models but also created fleets and hired and trusted younger people to drive the cars, he could not bring himself to do the same. His basic flaw was that he distrusted everybody, himself included.

Second of all, he did not appreciate his family life. He did not treasure his wife and much less his four children whom he tended to regard as burdens. It must be pointed out that in the 1920s and early 1930s, when his four children were born, they were not always welcomed as they came into this world. In this regard Virgínio, born in 1902, was a product of his generation. Wives were little more than maids who cooked and kept the house clean for their husbands and, whenever they wanted, were also the object of their carnal pleasures. Children, especially girls, would have been regarded as pit holes, good for nothing, who existed solely to help their mother serve the sole breadwinner of the household, the master.

Thirdly, he was jealous of others' successes, especially his own brother's acquired wealth that had come about as a result of a major Air France airplane disaster, that of a Lockheed L-749A Constellation, that crashed into Pico Redondo, close to Pico da Vara, the highest mountain in São Miguel at 1105m, flying from Paris to New York with a scheduled stopover in Santa Maria, on the night of October 28th, 1949. His brother Jaime had been responsible for making the lead coffins for all 48 passengers and crew who had perished in the disaster including, among others, the great boxer Marcel Cerdan, one of Edith Piaf's lovers, if not the most significant one. The journalist Eurico Mendes, writing in the *Diário dos Açores*, in its edition of November 1st, 2022, marked the 73rd anniversary of the tragedy and related how the tremendous noise resulting from the crash awoke many of the people living in the nearby villages of Santo António Nordestinho, Algarvia and Santana who then proceeded to ascend the mountain to find out what had happened and who, coming upon the horrific scene, took advantage of it by cutting some of the victims' fingers to extract their rings, an action that prompted the French authorities to label the local peasants *piratas de pé descalço*, that is to say barefooted pirates. Also, Mr. Mendes mentions that it was believed that the aircraft was carrying a lot of wrist watches and that the precious cargo vanished into thin air. Unhappy with the results of the local police investigation of the accident, the French government eventually sent in its own team of police officers to go from house to house in search of the stolen jewelry and watches. Lamentably, their intervention came only a few days after the crash and, therefore, met with limited success. Miraculously, whatever treasures the aircraft was carrying had quickly disappeared into thin air. Tragedies, as we have seen time and again throughout history, can bring both the best and the worst in people.

But there is more to Virgínio's flaws, when Elzira married António, his son-in-law's carefree lifestyle, his popularity and the respect that people displayed towards him regularly became a source of resentment for him, too. And, when António succumbed to the pure whim in April of 1961 of purchasing an Omega Seamaster gold wristwatch and bracelet, luxury items that cost a small fortune at the time and ones that only very well-off people could possibly envisage acquiring in an act of self-indulgence, Virgínio became even more envious of António and his possessions, especially that particular one. So, as soon as he found out that his son-in-law had died in America, the first thought that occurred to him was the gold watch. From that moment onwards he dreamt of one day wearing it himself.

Well, that opportunity presented itself in the spring of 1962 when António's belongings were finally returned from Boston to Ponta

Delgada. The most expensive item that he had possessed, the gold Omega Seamaster wristwatch, miraculously, had survived his demise and was among his personal items. It was a miracle that it had not been stolen in New York in the middle of the confusion at the Paramount Hotel where he had died. It's hard to believe that nobody realized its true value at the time. But Virgínio had an eye on the Omega Seamaster wristwatch and, at the first opportunity, he asked Elzira if he could wear it. Because she was living in his house for free and, therefore, at his mercy, and because he was helping her finalize her husband's unfinished business dealings, she reluctantly agreed to it. Before long, suspicious as he was, he thought that someone in America must have realized the true value of the watch and, therefore, must have changed the gold mechanism inside the watch's case and replaced it with a much less expensive one. So, instead of taking the watch to the jewelry store where it had been purchased, he decided to open its case himself on the kitchen table by means of a screwdriver and a hammer damaging it forever. When Elzira realized what he was up to, she nearly lost it and quickly and angrily took the watch away from him pointing out that one day it would be for me and that he was in the wrong for having damaged it in such a deliberate way. But it was too late, the damage to the watch was irreparable. Not long after that, he bought himself a wrist watch from a sailor in one of the ships that did the run between Lisbon and Ponta Delgada after being to Tenerife, in the Canary Islands. A watch that featured an automatic calendar, an innovation that the Seamaster did not have. He made it a point of showing it off to me so that I would think that my father's solid gold watch was not as good as his because it lacked the calendar.

On yet another occasion, to show his daughter that he had not forgotten the controversy and fiasco surrounding the Omega Seamaster wristwatch, he asked Elzira to lend him money to raise the backyard wall that separated the east side of his house from his neighbor's. For whatever reason, real or imaginary, he did not like the family living next door to him. Again, because she was not paying rent to live in his house, she felt compelled to help out by lending it to him. The debt, needless to say, was never paid back. And there were many other examples of his pettiness and plain nastiness. Virgínio, by the time he was in his fifties, had become a frustrated and bitter fellow as it will be further revealed in the next chapter. And yet, this is the same man, although reluctantly, who helped Elzira conclude António's business affairs, which proves that when all is said and done there were some flashes of goodness in him, too. Humans are indeed complex creatures.

27

Chaotic Burial Arrangements

As I have alluded to before, immediately upon hearing the news about António's premature demise, adult family members and close friends quickly came to the conclusion that something untoward had happened to him without having the necessary evidence to either prove or disprove their case. In other words, their belief was based on pure speculation and intuition. Irrespective, two theories soon emerged that were espoused, with rare exceptions, by people according to gender lines. The females blamed Laura for the tragedy while the males accused her old husband of having something to do with it. The former strongly felt that Laura, the adulteress, had exhausted António while the latter, a more rational group, was convinced that the so-called cuckold had poisoned the Azorean Casanova as retribution for having dishonored his good name and reputation. These conflicting theories gained further strength with the passage of time, and as a result of the contradictory information contained in Laura's letters to Elzira describing the sad events. They were further amplified by António's own letter written to her on August 20th in which he lies repeatedly about who had accompanied him to New York in a deliberate attempt to cover up the truth. In it, for instance, he claims that his friend, Mr. João Miranda, had accompanied him and Laura there when, in reality, he was not even aware that António was in America. Irrespective, nothing more was needed to trigger peoples' imagination back in remote São Miguel, an island so far away from the happening itself, in order for people to start weaving a story of their own making. America, after all, had the dubious reputation of being perceived among many as the land of gangsters, where law and order was absent in action.

After António's death one of the first priorities for his wife was to decide what to do with his remains. Was the corpse going to be transported back to São Miguel, or was it going to be buried in the US? Elzira and the rest of his family were leaning towards the former because it was his birthplace and because they thought that the funeral would be less expensive in Ponta Delgada while Laura, Aníbal and their friends in America preferred the latter. Burying him in New York City would be out of the question since none of António's friends and acquaintances lived there. In addition, buying a plot in a local cemetery would have been prohibitive. Laura's idea was to bring the body back to Boston, where most of the people he knew actually lived, and where the Jesse family already owned a plot at the Cambridge Cemetery. During the discussions that ensued between António's family and Laura about the matter, she went so far as to state that António was not a *cão*, a dog, to be sent by ship to São Miguel, which had been the initial decision made by his family. In any case, after the autopsy was completed, and while waiting for a final decision to be made by the family concerning burial arrangements, the corpse was being held momentarily at one of New York City's several morgues.

As pointed out in the previous chapter, a Power of Attorney had to be sent by Elzira enabling Laura to take care of the funeral and this took a few days before it got to her. In the meantime, thanks solely to the intervention of the Consul General of Portugal in New York, and the Portuguese Consulate's lawyer, Dr. Jerome Teich, the body was released on August 26th by the State of New York. If it were not for their personal intervention in this matter with the local authorities, after being asked by the Governor in Ponta Delgada to do so, the cadaver would have been held in place for six months. A long time indeed before closure could be achieved by all people concerned, those in São Miguel and the ones in America. So, as a direct consequence of António being a Portuguese government civil servant, and against all odds, the New York authorities had relented and released the body. It seems that working for the government does have some unforeseen advantages after all because, in the end, António's remains were sent by train to Boston before a copy of the Power of Attorney ever got to its final destination, the Portuguese Consulate and the local authorities in New York. All in all, it took four days for the body to be finally released to the Joseph A. Costa Sons Memorial Funeral Home in Cambridge in order for the funeral arrangements to proceed.

The wake itself went on for two days, on Monday and Tuesday, September 28th and 29th. And from all accounts, it was well attended by his friends and acquaintances. Also in attendance were Carl and Anthony Lo Conte, two individuals that António had met personally in 1960 and, again, just recently in 1961. They represented the branch of the Boston Musolino Co. and they showed up to pay their final respects to a man whom they had come to admire and respect as a business associate, and to offer Laura their help in view of finalizing António's business dealings with them as expeditiously as possible for the benefit of António's widow and young son. Many people sent flowers and all were very saddened by his sudden and untimely death. They took advantage of the moment to share with one another many of António's personal qualities and their individual connection with him.

According to Laura, her cousins thought that it would be a good idea if, in the name of the widow, flowers were displayed on top of the coffin. They also thought that António's son should do the same. To that end, Laura ordered a basket of flowers in Elzira's name and a flower arrangement in the shape of a heart covered with white and red carnations on top of which one could read on full display my name and hers. Was it a Freudian slip on her part? Why would she want to display so publicly and so prominently her own name when she clearly did not belong to António's immediate family? If anything, the red and white flower arrangement in the shape of a heart should have been reserved for Elzira and me, not herself. In any case, Laura's decision at the time was fodder for much talk and speculation, especially for my mother, her parents and her two brothers about the real relationship that seemed to have existed between her husband and the adulteress.

After mass at 9 o'clock at St. Anthony's Church in Somerville on Wednesday, August 30th, the interment took place at the Cambridge Cemetery. The last eight days had been an ordeal for all concerned, those in the US, and those far away, in Ponta Delgada, especially the latter, who found it daunting to visualize all the goings on in a country with such unusual customs when it came to burying its dead. As a souvenir, one of António's friends thought of shooting a short film at the wake as well as at the exit from St. Anthony's Church for the benefit of his family, especially my mother and me. Eventually, we, that is to say António's closest family, watched that dreadful short film in the summer of 1962. While we watched it in complete silence, it still seemed unreal to all of us that António's death had actually taken place because it was in a movie. Especially, closure did not come easily for my mother and me. It took years for the concept of this distant death to sink in firmly in our brains.

Just recently, in 2020, I asked a talented photography technician to convert the contents of the fragile 8 mm film into a DVD disk. Sixty years had gone by since I had watched it for the first time but the experience was just as poignant. The recording of António's funeral lasts a total of six minutes. Once again, I watched carefully the wake at the funeral parlor and, afterwards, the casket being carried from St. Anthony's Church to the hearse waiting by the curb in front of the church. At the funeral parlor the film focuses mostly on António lying in the coffin which is covered and surrounded by flowers and then the camera slowly pans so that the viewer can see the mourners in attendance, especially Laura. At the exit from St. Anthony's, the amateur film maker shoots the scene from across the street. And, as people start streaming out of the church behind the coffin, one can spot a very tearful Laura, a woman devasted by the loss of someone who was so dear to her heart and, beside her, walking expressionless, her old husband.

In 1961, the total expenses for the funeral amounted to $900.36 USD. An enormous amount by Portuguese standards at the time. At a rate of exchange of 28$52 *escudos* per dollar, which was the average then, it totaled the sum of 25 678$26 *escudos*. It was an amount unheard of in Ponta Delgada and one that distressed the poor widow who did not have much money to spare. And, according to Laura, the price had been more than reasonable because it was a direct consequence of the Jesses' friendship with the owner and a personal favor of his to a family who had given the Costa Funeral Home lots of business in the past. By comparison, Elzira's own funeral costs in 1981, twenty years later, in Ponta Delgada, were only 81 331$00 *escudos*.

As Calderón himself would have said it, António's life had been a *frenesí*, and an *ilusión*. For the last couple of years, he had been so busy trying to establish the export business, which would have paved the way out of his ordinary lifestyle, that he had not paid much attention to any negative impact that all that stress was having on his health. The stress, coupled with the fact that he had been a heavy smoker since his teenage years, made for a deadly combination, to be sure. That said, his immediate family, especially Elzira, did not believe that he had died of natural causes because it had happened almost immediately upon arriving in America. And, when the results of the autopsy were divulged, they only added to the suspicion that he had been the target of some perverse scheme.

In his last few conscious moments at the Paramount Hotel, in a strange city and even a stranger hotel room, in the arms of a woman who was not his wife, he must have realized that all his efforts had been in vain and, consequently, an *ilusión*. Did he have any regrets? As an intelligent and experienced human being, he must have realized the gravity of his predicament and that his chances of surviving whatever health problems he was having were slim and that, therefore, he probably would never see his wife and son again.

Laura states in her second letter that just before he passed away, he tried to tell her something but that he was already unable to speak. Did he want to entrust her with a special message for his young son who was going to be fatherless, just like he had been? Did it occur to him that I was only nine and would have to go through the same difficult times that he had experienced himself as a child? Or, conversely, were his last thoughts directed at Elzira, his supportive wife who had done everything in her power to make life pleasant for him and given him a wonderful child? Was he afraid of dying? I have wondered many times about what those last words would have been if he had had a chance to utter them and if they had been repeated faithfully to his family. Sadly, however, I will never know the message that they would have conveyed because he never got to say them. That said, I have entertained many possible ideas as to what António's last thoughts would have been.

My father loved me deeply and he just knew, in his moment of agony, that he would not be there to protect his most treasured possession, me, in the years to come. History was going to repeat itself whether he liked it or not and there was nothing he could do to counteract the forces of destiny and somehow escape death. No one ever escapes death. When the time comes, one just goes. It is reasonable to believe that António's last thoughts were perhaps directed at me for a very good reason. According to the notes that he left behind for Elzira, he was totally convinced that she would be financially independent and, consequently, in a position, when I finished high school, to finance my university studies without difficulty in Continental Portugal. This was António's biggest dream for me. As for my mother, she was an adult and, therefore, less vulnerable than I would ever be to face the vicissitudes of fortune. As it turned out, how wrong all his financial planning proved to be! In reality, Elzira was left in a bind after his death, and had to fight for every single *escudo* just to make ends meet and provide the necessities of life for herself and me.

In *All the Devils Are Here* by Louise Penny, Armand Gamache, speaking candidly to his second-in-command, Jean-Guy Beauvoir, who happens to be also his son-in-law and whose wife is about to give birth any day to a daughter with Down syndrome, he says: "We're all afraid. Of something bad happening to our children. Of not being there when they need us. Of not being enough." Jean-Guy is worried and suffering from anxiety because he does not know if he will be up to the challenge of caring for someone like his daughter for the rest of his life and hers. Armand reassures him that he will be up to the task, that he will rise to the occasion. In his last moments of consciousness, António found himself in a similar predicament as Jean-Guy but with one obvious difference, he had run out of time.

# THREE

Life After the Tragedy

28

Living with a Bully Again!

Elzira had to rely on her father's help to liquidate the business mess left behind by António. That entailed a lot of correspondence back and forth between her, the Musolino Co. and Laura, the woman that Elzira perceived as the cause of her own personal misfortune and someone not to be trusted. Numerous arguments and discussions took place late at night between father and daughter until the end of 1962 when, finally, António's business affairs and funeral costs were settled once and for all putting an end to a very dark period in her life. I, who slept on the ground floor, directly underneath the dining room where the conversations took place, used to fall asleep listening to them and, to this day, the words *Musolino* and *White*, not to mention *Laura* and *Aníbal*, conjure up all sorts of images related to my father's disappearance from my life.

In the meantime, my mother was the subject of ridicule and put downs by her father who had read the love letters between her husband and Laura. Henceforth, he never wasted an opportune moment to bring to her attention that all the trouble that she was facing, and him, indirectly, was a direct consequence of her husband's infidelity. In his eyes, the man whose lifestyle he had envied had become a source of scorn because of his short-lived peccadillo. Daily life was definitely unpleasant for Elzira at this point.

Virgínio's behavior, from what I am about to relate, leads one to conclude that deep down he was not a very honorable fellow. Case in point: he did not hesitate to take full advantage of the opportunity that Elzira had moved into his home, albeit at his own invitation, to benefit financially from the situation. In late 1962, at the conclusion of António's business affairs, she had been left with enough money to live a modest life and to take care of my growing financial needs as I was about to enroll in high school. Virgínio had intimate knowledge of every cent and dime that Elzira had in her bank account. After all, the two of them had dealt with all her financial matters ever since António's passing. The problem was that she had been left with more money than he had expected. He thought, perhaps, that she would share willingly with him most of it in which case he would live a rather worry-free life going forward. Unfortunately for him, however, Elzira had other plans for that money; she intended to save as much of it as possible for my university education to carry out her husband's wish. Still, from time to time, Virgínio borrowed money from her and it was never paid back. So, technically, Elzira was not living for free in his home. Besides, my mother was the one who bought groceries for herself and me. Basically, the two of us occupied only one room on the ground floor, a room that was not being used anyways in Virgínio's home. And yet, despite all the conflicts that came about because of his interference in all aspects of our daily life, the man, like most human beings, was capable of displaying flashes of kindness and friendship towards me on occasion.

On Sundays, after lunch, when it was time to return to his spot at the taxi stand that in those days was all around Igreja da Matriz (Main Church), also called Igreja de São Sebastião (San Sebastian's Church), the patron saint of Ponta Delgada, he used to put my bicyclc in his cab's trunk and drop me off at the eastern end of Avenida Marginal, also called Avenida Infante Dom Henrique, so that I would not have to bicycle all the way to get there, for an afternoon of bicycling with a few other boys of my age. The sidewalk at the Avenida was the widest in Ponta Delgada and the flattest and, therefore, a favorite spot for any boy with a pair of wheels. Riding at top speed back and forth on the flat sidewalk of the Avenida when the weather was good, of course, was a most enjoyable pastime. And, less frequently, when Virgínio had to take a fare to some place on the north side of the island, he would take me along, with the customer's consent, of course, for the ride. It was a fun way to discover the beautiful Azorean countryside.

But, in spite of these extraordinary and rare acts of kindness and goodwill, it was his daily behavior in between them that defined eventually the man. His constant verbal abuse of his wife and widowed daughter left a bittersweet taste in the mouth of those who had to live with him and, by the time I became a teenager, when I had lost most of my childhood naivety, I saw the man for what he was, a bully. To sum up, the everyday living conditions under Virgínio's roof left a lot to be desired for both my mother and me.

Irrespective, she, in spite of it all, was determined to carry on and see to it that I would be protected and have the educational opportunities that António had wished for me. Her commitment to this cause never wavered for the next seventeen years, that is to say, until I graduated with an Honors B.A. from Saint Michael's College at the University of Toronto in 1977. She must have breathed a sigh of relief the day that she attended my convocation and received that first degree, which was quickly followed by a second one, a B.Ed., also from the same university. Mission accomplished, she probably thought to herself! Had she not passed away on November 19th, 1981, she would have been very pleased to find out that those two degrees were eventually followed by another two: an M.A. and a Ph.D. from my alma mater. As for António, I think that he would have been proud of my academic and professional accomplishments. He would have been even more impressed to learn that I had accomplished them in a foreign country and in a language other than Portuguese. He would have felt vindicated in his firm belief that an education opens many doors and is one of the keys to a gratifying and, hopefully, happy life. In retrospective, thanks to António's dream of a university education for me, I enjoyed a wonderful and very fulfilling career in the field of education for thirty-nine years and, in turn, made sure that my own daughter would benefit from the same academic opportunities that were available to me, which she has, having graduated herself from the same university as me with an Honors B.A. and a Master degree in Forest Conservation.

That said, from August 22nd, 1961, to December 22nd, 1969, the day that both my mother and I boarded an airplane in Santa Maria destined to Toronto, there were many challenges and obstacles to overcome for the two of us in Ponta Delgada and, for Elzira in particular, there must have been many moments of doubt regarding whether she would live long enough to carry out her husband's last wishes. Moments of doubt that increased significantly once in Canada, a country totally unfamiliar to her, a country whose two official languages, English and French, she did not understand in the least. The numerous challenges that lay ahead would require nothing short of a leap of faith on her part that, eventually, everything would turn out all right. She was convinced that the sacrifice she was making was well worth it. She was emigrating to Canada to save me from being drafted into the Portuguese army and, almost certainly, being sent to Africa to fight in a colonial war of attrition where one of her own brothers, Francisco, a military career man, had completed several tours of duty, and who had been lucky enough to live to tell the story, fortunately. It's to her credit that she found within herself the unselfish drive to overcome courageously most of the adversities that she encountered in her new country and, for that, I will remain eternally grateful to her.

29

Laura's Nineteen Letters to Elzira in 1961-62

For anyone who takes the time to investigate someone's past, personal letters are precious documents, especially the ones written by individuals who have long ceased to live and, consequently, are no longer here to answer any possible questions that the researcher may have dealing with particular aspects of that person's life. The work of the individual charged with the task of examining old documents is very much like the work of a private detective who tries to figure out the motives that led someone to commit murder when the murderer and the victim are both dead and, therefore, unable to shed some light on the case. In spite of this obvious drawback, inevitably, personal letters reveal, or hide, a lot about their authors and the people referenced and described in them; Laura's letters are no exception to this rule. As one reads and rereads them carefully, looking for tidbits of pertinent information, searching for obvious or somewhat camouflaged contradictions that may occur without the writer being aware of them, one begins to develop in one's mind a picture of the kind of person that she was in 1960-1961, how she perceived António, how she dealt with the event itself of António's death given that she was the only live witness present when it happened and, finally, how she faced, going forward, the outcome of the tragedy.

There were nineteen letters written by Laura to Elzira between August 26th, 1961, and November 22nd, 1962, when the correspondence between them ceased altogether. The bulk of these letters, thirteen, to be exact, were written between August 30th and December 15th, 1961, during a very short period of time. By far the most important one, and the longest, is her second letter which has been referenced from time to time thus far on account of its significance; it is the letter in which she describes in great detail António's death at the Paramount Hotel in New York.

Aside from these nineteen letters to Elzira, there were another six sent to her father, Virgínio. Some of these, too, go on for several pages and provide a wealth of information and detail about what occurred in New York and, in particular, about António's unfinished business dealings and how they were progressing during the last quarter of 1961 and throughout 1962. Besides these twenty-five letters, there were also several telegrams written right after António's death dealing with the Power of Attorney that Laura needed to receive from Elzira in order to deal with the funeral arrangement issue.

Laura's letters to Elzira are written in Portuguese. Her knowledge of the language is typical of that of an immigrant who left the Azores with an elementary school education and was exposed to another language, in this case English, from the moment of her arrival in America onwards. Although she can and does express herself reasonably well, she makes a lot of spelling and grammar mistakes which, at times, impede comprehension of the information that she is trying to convey. As for her mastery of English, it is also typical of someone who did not study it formally in the US. It was picked up orally through daily contact with, most likely, her husband and son and, of course, other immigrants who did not possess a good command of it. In spite of these obvious shortcomings, her letters provide a wealth of information and insight into "António's case".

In almost all of the letters, Laura addresses Elzira as if she were a friend in distress and, in one of them, she goes so far as to call her a "sister" with a common purpose: to work together for my benefit. She mentions several times that António was constantly speaking about me in loving terms and that he had told her that he was working hard to make sure that my future would be better than his own. She also finishes most of them by sending a hug for Elzira and kisses for me.

Elzira, on the other hand, seems to have mistrusted Laura's motives, honesty and moral integrity right from the beginning of their correspondence, especially when it came to solving successfully the unfinished money transactions with the Musolino Co. Although she did not keep any rough copies of her own letters to Laura that would prove unequivocally her misgivings about Laura's intentions, one is forced to arrive at this unavoidable conclusion based on the number of times that Laura had to explain the business details in her own letters to her. Unhappily for Laura, after Elzira received posthumously António's letter dated August 20th, in which he mentions repeatedly that his friend, Mr. João Miranda, accompanied them to New York, and Laura's second letter in which she does not mention Mr. João Miranda not even once, she started to put two and two together as to what had been going on between her husband and Laura. Finally, her suspicions were proved correct when the stash of love letters from Laura was discovered inside one of the drawers in António's desk at the Governo Civil and handed to her father who, eventually, handed it to his grieving daughter. My mother was heartbroken. She had been betrayed by her husband. That said, in her mind, the real culprit remained the temptress, the seductress, the whore, Laura. She was, therefore, blamed for the tragedy in Elzira's mind. So, how could she possibly entrust her son's future and her own to someone who had betrayed her?

Regardless of Elzira's deep-rooted negative feelings towards Laura for her perceived part in António's demise, the letters reveal that Laura seems to be genuinely sorry for the widow's predicament and concerned about her financial well-being going forward. To that end, she vowed to help the two of us as best she could. Was she doing this favor out of the guilt feelings that she was harboring for her part in the tragedy? What is known for sure is that at the funeral parlor, in front of several witnesses, in true melodramatic fashion, she promised out loud, so that people in the immediate vicinity could bear witness, to assist my mother and me in any way that she possibly could if for no other reason than to satisfy António's soul, as she put it.

Starting with her first letter, dated August 26th, 1961, four days after António's death, Laura says to the stricken widow who was desperate to know details about the tragedy:

Elzira, ainda hoje não te posso contar como foi a sua morte porque só a ideia me horrorisa e deixa desolada. Aníbal sofreu o choque e ainda sofre; até não sei como está trabalhando.

(Elzira, as of today I still cannot tell you how he died because just the idea horrifies me and leaves me grieved. Aníbal suffered the shock and he is still suffering; I do not even know how he is working.)

The entire ordeal in New York must have been a true nightmare for her who was not psychologically prepared to deal with such an unexpected turn of events. Is anyone ever ready to face such a catastrophe and deal with its fallout? Let's face it, she would have a lot of explaining to do to the cops once they would take over the investigation of the circumstances leading to the poor fellow's death. They probably would want to know what a married woman from Boston was doing in a hotel room in New York with a man who was not her husband and who had just died. It would not be farfetched to believe that their preliminary conclusion was that she was a prostitute.

The immediate consequences for Laura upon returning home from New York were that she admits to be on the brink of a nervous breakdown. She lies awake at night just thinking about António's death. She also knows that she will have a lot of explaining to do to his loved ones back in São Miguel, and to his friends and acquaintances in the US, too. Indeed, she did have good reasons to feel apprehensive and nervous.

She also reveals, in this first letter and subsequent ones, her religious beliefs, something that was predictable due to the fact that she was born in 1926 in an ultraconservative catholic Ponta Delgada. She says:

Elzira, tem forças, pede a Deus que te dê resignação, porque eu dou o valor ao que estás passando com a falta de António, e pede a Deus [que] me dê forças para terminar com o resto dos negócios para benefício do Roberto e teu.

(Elzira, be strong, ask God for resignation, because I understand what you are going through with António's absence, and ask God to give me strength to finish the rest of the business dealings for your benefit and Roberto's.)

That said, this reference to God catches one a bit off guard because it's coming from a woman who was having an illicit affair and whose moral rectitude was thus somewhat compromised. She finishes the letter by coming back to the idea that Elzira must accept God's wishes, an idea that will be reiterated in other letters as well. It is also of interest to note that Laura is asking the widow to pray God to give her enough strength to bring to a successful conclusion the business transactions that António had undertaken, and which she claims were almost completed by himself. She tells Elzira, therefore, not to worry about them because it's just a question of time before she will receive the balance of the money. And towards the end of the letter, she states:

Mas repito, se te puder auxiliar em qualquer coisa para teu benefício e do Roberto, não hesites. Pelo menos permita Deus que sirva para descanso da sua alma porque em vida só pensava no conforto de vocês, e no futuro do Roberto.

(I repeat, if I can help you in whatever way for your benefit and Roberto's, do not hesitate [to ask]. God willing, it will serve for the repose of his soul because, while alive, he only thought of your comfort, and of Roberto's future.)

She appears to be offering her help and services as a form of personal redemption. According to her, it was the least that she could do for my mother and me.

When it comes to the content of the second letter, the one dealing with the circumstances surrounding António's final moments, the devil is really in its details because there are contradictions with regards to the unfolding of the events in New York. For instance, were António and Laura sharing a room at the Paramount Hotel or did they have separate ones? According to Laura's version of the facts, they had separate rooms and she describes how António, feeling sick, knocks at her door at 6:15 in the morning of August 22nd asking for aspirins. He does not look like his usual self. She notices right away that he has not combed his hair and that he is barefoot. He seems to be in great distress. She gives him two aspirins. He runs to the bathroom to get a glass of water. He is only able to swallow the first one. He is still able to speak clearly at this point. He asks her to call a doctor right away because he feels awful. Laura says that right after this request, he returned to his room while she called the reception. A couple of minutes later Laura, worried, and not wanting him to be alone, leaves her room to go to his but finds him in the corridor unable to get into his own room because he had left the key inside and the doors at most hotels, as everyone knows, lock automatically for security purposes. She brings him back to her own room and says that he was reluctant to do so because she was in pajamas (she had taken no luggage with her at all thinking that they would be back in Boston that very evening! So, where did the pajamas come from?). However, she persuades him to come in and he does so where a few moments later he dies in her arms while sitting on the edge of her bed unable to breathe. As he was expiring, he still tried to tell her something that was quite important to him, but the words were never uttered. She noticed at this point that his heart had stopped beating. That's when she started screaming for help. Seconds later, she was surrounded by all sorts of hotel guests, employees and police officers.

This description of events, nevertheless, is proved wrong by the fact that there was only one bill for a room at the Paramount Hotel. Why would she feel compelled to elaborate such a detailed and, actually, convincing tale? There is only one plausible explanation that makes sense: it was done in order to cover that the two of them were sharing the same room and that they were having an affair.

But there is more to the story that Laura is weaving so realistically. António's only letter to his wife during the 1961 trip was written on Sunday, August 20th, as I have mentioned several times before. He wrote it from the Jesse residence in Somerville. In it, he clearly states that the following day, Monday, he, Laura and Mr. João Miranda would be returning to New York and that, furthermore, the three of them had already been there on Thursday, Friday and on Saturday morning of the previous week and that they had returned to Boston because nothing else could be accomplished in New York during the weekend. In addition, he goes so far as to state that his friend's presence is making life difficult for him and for the positive outcome of the business meetings with the New Yorkers. He specifically blames Mr. João Miranda's mediocre knowledge of English for some of the difficulties in the negotiations. He was finding fault now, in 1961, with the same man who had taken the time to travel with him to New York in the summer of 1960!

Desde quarta-feira que, minto, desde quinta-feira até ontem, estive em New York. Têm-me acompanhado a Laura e o João Miranda. Este é um trapalhão muito grande a falar o inglês, mas a Laura, que o fala muitíssimo bem, é que me tem salvo de situações que me poderiam prejudicar. Tem sido incansável. O marido também estava para ir connosco a New York, mas como esteve doente aqueles 4 meses, disse-me que lhe era totalmente impossível deslocar-se nesta altura, para não ter que fechar mais uma vez a barbearia.

Amanhã, voltamos os 3 novamente a New York e espero voltar ainda mesmo amanhã, se as coisas correrem bem.

Apesar do João Miranda se encontrar com a melhor disposição em me ajudar, ele está-me a complicar a vida porque sempre quer que os 100 sacos e, estou mesmo a ver que vai ser fiado. Enfim, Deus há-de permitir que as coisas hão-de correr pelo melhor.

(From Wednesday, I lie, from Thursday until yesterday, I was in New York. Laura and João Miranda have been with me. The latter is a huge blunderer when speaking English, but Laura, who speaks exceptionally well, is the one who has saved me from situations that could have negatively affected me. She has been tireless. Her husband was also supposed to accompany us to New York, but because of his four-month long illness, he told me that it was impossible for him to do so at this time so that he would not have to close again the barber shop.

Tomorrow, the three of us will go back to New York and I hope to return [to Boston] tomorrow if everything runs smoothly.

Even though João Miranda has the best of intentions to help me, he is complicating my life because he still wants the 100 bags and I can see that it's going to be for free. To sum up, God willing, everything will turn out fine.)

Well, well, well, it turns out that Mr. João Miranda never accompanied António and Laura to New York before and after that weekend in August of 1961. In fact, he did not even know that his friend was in the US. So, António was deliberately hiding from his wife that the only person who did accompany him on the two trips was Laura, and he did it for obvious reasons. He did not want his wife to know about it. She would have interpreted it as a clear indication that he was having an affair with Laura and as a sign of his disloyalty and unfaithfulness.

We all know that people, man and women alike, can be quite creative when it comes to covering up extramarital affairs. António was drawing her attention to something that clearly never had taken place as a distractive tactic. That is what he was attempting to do so that he would not create suspicions in Elzira's mind that something unusual was going on between him and Laura, which is what would have happened if he were to openly admit that she had been the only one who had gone with him to New York. In other words, he was deliberately creating a false narrative. Unfortunately for António, he was caught with the hand in the cookie jar and died before having some serious explaining to do about his actions and deeds in America. As one says in the theater world, he exited stage right in a hurry leaving a lot of unanswered questions and a multitude of loose ends to be knotted by those left behind on the grand stage of life.

All this brings me to the following observation: Laura's personality and her actions and reactions throughout and after the ordeal of António's passing were not only shaped by her Azorean background, that is to say her immediate family, education, health status and the physical environment that was part and parcel of her daily life in Ponta Delgada during her formative years, but also, later on, as a young adult, by her adopted community of Somerville, in the US. She was influenced by her interactions with it and by her fellow immigrants and, inevitably, as time went on, by some American ideas and culture. Therefore, by Azorean standards, the Laura that António met in America in 1960 was very different from the vast majority of Azorean women. She would have been considered quite liberal by her counterparts in São Miguel. She had evolved differently due to the fact that she had been exposed to a variety of different factors in America that were simply non-existent in the Azores. That's perhaps, after all, what attracted António to her. That said, she remained in many ways a naïve woman and a dreamer.

In that regard Laura is, for instance, stunned to discover that António had Azorean business associates who had invested considerable sums of money into the export business. This is especially hard for her to swallow because she had translated throughout 1961 all of his correspondence, not to mention, of course, that António and her had

had, in the summer of 1960, countless opportunities to discuss face to face the ins and outs of the export business. Was she blinded by love? After his death, the lack of transparency on António's part leaves her bewildered. She had been under the impression all along that he was acting alone and that there were no business partners. She had no clue that they existed. Suddenly, she was told that there were several people in the background. She quickly found out that Mr. Dinis Mota Soares, Mr. Manuel Rodrigues Castelo, Mr. Eduardo Valério and others were some of them. She was dismayed and shocked by this news.

It is noteworthy to point out that António never revealed to her this most important aspect of the business. Had he been transparent about it, he would not have been perceived in such a favorable light by her, I am afraid. He wanted to impress this woman by showing off, and by creating the illusion that he was the only person in charge. In any case, it was deceitful of him to deliberately hide this piece of information from her. It reveals that even the most honest person can, and frequently does, from time to time, lie openly about the truth or deliberately avoids it out of vanity and a false sense of pride.

People are complex creatures. Their actions and reactions reveal both a mixture of weaknesses and personality flaws, and strengths and outstanding qualities. To keep a balance between these opposing forces during one's life constitutes a major challenge. For António, however, his need to impress Laura at any cost, so it seems, by pretending to be the sole proprietor of the business venture, led him to be deliberately opaque about the existence of partners. For her part, Laura was so taken by his presence that she neglected asking all sorts of pertinent questions that should have been asked. Based on her superficial knowledge of the business, she made the erroneous assumption that António was acting alone.

That said, because she had some inside knowledge about António's business thanks to the translations and the odd telephone call that she had made to the Musolino Co. on his behalf, she felt that she had what it took to bring about a satisfactory conclusion to what he had not had time to finish in New York. But, in order to be able to do so confidently and efficiently, she demanded that Elzira be honest about António's business partners in São Miguel. Elzira had no problem doing just that.

In the meantime, some of these gentlemen wasted no time in contacting Laura directly once they found out that their point man in America had passed away bypassing, in the process, the widow altogether who lived in the same city as they did and who could be easily reached had they wanted to get in touch with her. They were in panic mode. *Sauve-qui-peut*, helter-skelter flight on their part. They were looking out for their self-interests first and foremost, of course, and trying to salvage whatever money they had invested in the enterprise. However, by acting independently from one another they created a lot of confusion as to who owed money to whom.

For Laura, once she was informed of the identity of the business associates, it was a question of pressing the Musolino Co. to pay whatever it still owed António for the fava beans. Nevertheless, because some of the bags had been sold on a consignment basis, it meant that the company could only pay for their sale as they were being sold, something that Elzira never quite understood in spite of Laura's multiple explanations, and that frustrated her enormously. My mother wanted quick results. She wanted to conclude all aspects of António's business and move on to focus on me and secure my future whose success was now in doubt.

But, in spite of Laura's best efforts, it took over one year for the Musolino Co. to pay Elzira the balance of the money that it owed her which was a fraction of the real value of the merchandise because the company claimed that the product had become stale with the passage of time. The Musolino Co. was not about to absorb a loss to help out the poor widow and her young son. Business is business! That said, it remains true that Laura was tireless and relentless in trying to bring to a conclusion António's unfinished business in America. She made many calls on Elzira's behalf to both the Boston and New York headquarters of the Musolino Co. before she could breathe a sigh of relief when it was all over. Finally, in November of 1962, her part in the saga was over. She had kept her word given out loud at the funeral parlor.

From a purely business perspective, had António not mixed pleasure with work, he would have been quite successful within a few years for he had discovered a gold mine in the export of Azorean products to America. He had the drive, the perseverance, the know-how, and the interpersonal skills necessary to succeed in a tough world. In other words, he was a very motivated businessman. He was also a risk taker, a critical personality trait for any aspiring entrepreneur. All signs pointed to the real chance that by the age of fifty or so he would have achieved his goal of financial freedom had he not perished. That, however, was not to be.

The autopsy results are addressed in Laura's ninth letter to Elzira. She seems to be aware that many people in Ponta Delgada thought that António had been poisoned to death in America. She declares:

Como vês na Certidão de Óbito, António faleceu por causa da garganta. Agora que fiquen descansados, que foi por morte natural e não como diziam. Elzira, desculpa em eu falar assim, mas eu fico brava com esta gente daí que está sempre a pensar naquilo que não é.

(As you can see from the Death Certificate, António died because of the throat [edema of the larynx]. I hope this will suffice to stop the gossiping; it was on account of natural causes and not as people were claiming. Elzira, excuse me for speaking like this, but I get mad with the folks [in São Miguel] who are always imagining things that are not true.)

Laura is referring to the legitimate autopsy, done in New York, which determined that António's cause of death was laryngeal edema, a swelling of the throat that prevented him from swallowing and breathing properly, accompanied by an abscess of the peritoneum which is normally caused by bacteria. To put it bluntly, he suffocated to death. She underlines key words in the letter to categorically point out that she had absolutely nothing to do with his death, contrary to popular opinion in Ponta Delgada. And in her last words she accuses the people of São Miguel of being in the habit of *espalhar boatos*, creating rumors, without possessing the true facts to substantiate their opinions. She blames Azoreans for being narrow minded and gossipers of the worst kind.

So, the autopsy results seem to confirm and validate the symptoms that António started experiencing on Sunday night, August 20th, at the Jesse home, and which progressively got worse on Monday. Yet, despite the official autopsy, Elzira, her family members and friends continued to believe that something perverse had happened to António, something that had caused his premature death. They continued to think that he had been poisoned. For the women, including Elzira, the main target of their suspicions was Laura, the temptress. The men, however, held a different opinion and pointed the accusatory finger at the old barber. According to them, if anybody had a good motive to seek revenge, it would have been him for being made a cuckold.

Another subject frequently addressed in many of the letters is António's personal belongings that had to be returned to Ponta Delgada at some point in time. Naturally, the widow wanted them back as soon as possible. However, here the challenge was finding an honest individual formerly from São Miguel who would be visiting his native island willing to assume the responsibility of delivering his suitcase with its valuable contents to Elzira. Finally, thanks to Laura's connections within the Portuguese community in Somerville, someone trustworthy was found and my mother received in April of 1962 my father's suitcase with his belongings and the gifts that he had purchased for her and me and for some of his friends at the Governo Civil.

The arrival of António's suitcase was another bittersweet moment for the two of us. We suddenly came to the realization that António had in fact died and was never going to return from America. It provided a form of closure. His belongings remained for many years a constant reminder of the man that he had been because they were not disposed of immediately. The suits were hung inside the wardrobe and his personal items such as wallets, fountain pens, rings and the Omega Seamaster 18-Karat gold wristwatch were carefully kept by Elzira in her chest of drawers for my eventual use. It is most ironic that the one piece of fine jewelry of which António was most proud, the Omega Seamaster, he only got to wear it for a few brief months. It had been purchased on April 25th, 1961, in Ponta Delgada, and on August 22nd, he was dead. Every once in a while, these personal items would come out of the drawers and I would see and touch them with a sense of awe. I was too young to use or wear any of them, objects that had defined the man, my father, who had vanished from my life so soon.

What Laura says about Elzira's decision to leave the Machado residence and move to her father's house comes up in her eleventh letter, dated November 15th, 1961. She asserts that it was a mistake on Elzira's part to move out. She states categorically that if she had been in her shoes, she would have never left the house. She points out that it was not Elzira's mother-in-law, the owner of the house, but rather her brother-in-law, José, who had kicked out my mother and me and that he was not in a position to do so. Regrettably, she was not aware that he was doing the dirty work for his mother. In any case, she does not mince words about expressing her opinions and shows as a result that she is a woman with strong convictions and an innate sense of fairness, the former being a personality trait that contrasts with Elzira's meekness. She is not afraid to take a stand even if it makes her disliked and unpopular in the eyes of others. She goes on to declare:

> *Eu parece-me que disse a teu pai, e também te digo, que foi um erro teres saído daquela casa. É verdade que não se pode viver com brigas, mas se eu estivesse no teu lugar, nunca saía da casa que o meu marido adorava, porque tenho impressão que outros vão gozar o que António fez lá em casa. Elzira, quero que me compreendas, eu não estou tirando parte por ninguém (quanto mais que ninguém me escreve a dizer nada talvez com receio que eu faça enredos, mas não sou rapariga de enredos; quando*

abro a minha boca é quando tenho a certeza do que estou a dizer embora leve anos para o fazer). Mas, voltando acima, digo-te que se tua sogra não te disse para saíres, para que fizeste caso do que José te disse? Terá ele mais direito do que tu de estares ali morando? Terá mais direito o filho dele que o teu filho? Desculpa-me, Elzira, de te falar desta maneira, mas eu sou sincera, e estou ficando brava da maneira como as coisas se estão passando. Explicaste-me os concertos que António tinha feito; António tinha-me contado tal qual como me disseste na tua carta. Sinto uma pena enorme de tudo isso se dar.

(It seems that I told your father, and I am telling you as well, that it was a mistake for you to leave that house [the Machado's house]. It's true that one cannot live with disputes, but if I were in your place, I would never have left the house that my husband loved, because I feel that others are going to enjoy what António did in it [the renovations]. Elzira, I want you to understand me, I am not siding with anyone (actually, no one writes to me telling me what is going on perhaps because they fear that I will create trouble, but I am not one to gossip; when I open my mouth is when I am sure of what I am saying even though it may take years for me to do it.

But, coming back to the above, I am telling you that if your mother-in-law did not tell you to leave, why did you pay attention to what José told you? Is he more entitled than you to be living there? Is his son more entitled than yours? Excuse me, Elzira, for speaking like this, but I am sincere, and I am mad about the turn of events. You explained to me the renovations that António had made; António had told me exactly the same. I am very sorry for what is going on.)

In the passage above, she also expresses her dismay for a family in disarray, a family that she had admired in the past because she thought that its members were united. *O hábito não faz o monge.* Appearances are deceiving.

In her fifteenth letter, dated April 19th, 1962, she expresses the regret that Elzira does not want to continue with the export business that António had started and that had so much potential. She suggests that if she lived in Ponta Delgada, surely the two of them would be able to forge ahead. By taking this stand, she shows that she is an intelligent, confident and an enterprising woman who knew that she had what it took to succeed in a sector that was totally dominated by men in the São Miguel of the early 1960s.

It is also significant to remark that in her correspondence she only mentions in passing her husband's feelings towards me and my particular predicament. She says, in her third letter, dated the same day as her second, that *Aníbal tem muita pena do Roberto porque ele [Aníbal] nunca teve carinho do pai*. (Aníbal pities Roberto because he himself was never loved by his father.) Besides, she states, this lack of love is something that had affected profoundly her husband all his life. So, he feels sorry for me because I won't experience anymore the love of my father. She comes back to the husband's feelings towards me again in her fifth letter, dated September 5th, 1961; she says that her husband: *Está sempre a falar nele [Roberto]; tem uma dor de ele ficar sem pai tão novinho que ninguém calcula*. (He is constantly speaking about him [Roberto]; nobody can imagine how sorry he is for Roberto losing his father so young.)

Are the old barber's feelings genuine or is he putting on an act? After all, as suggested elsewhere, he had good reasons to seek some sort of revenge for being made a fool by his wife and António. In other words, would the fact that António had a young son have been enough of a deterrent for him not to want to clear his good name and, in the process, teach the two "lovebirds" a lesson that they would not forget any time soon? *On ne voit bien qu'avec le cœur…*

On her seventeenth letter, dated April 2nd, 1962, she informs Elzira that she plans to visit São Miguel in 1963 and that she is looking forward to the opportunity to have a woman-to-woman chat with her about the entire ordeal. She states that she wants to clear any doubts in my mother's mind about her involvement, directly or indirectly, in António's death. Again, this points to the fact that she seems to be a woman who is not afraid to face a hostile audience, Elzira and her family, one that is convinced that she is guilty of seducing a married man while forgetting, conveniently, that he also played an active part in the affair himself. In any case, it would not have been the first time since emigrating to America that she would have returned to São Miguel.

As an aside, in one of the many family albums kept by my mother, there is a photograph of myself when I was five years old taken by Laura in the summer of 1957 when she visited her native São Miguel on vacation accompanied by her son and, perhaps, by her husband, too. Apparently, her son and I played together in spite of our age difference, something that I don't recall at all doing. Whether or not there were also contacts between António and Laura at the time is not known. That said, in a small city where everybody knew everybody, it is difficult to imagine how António and Laura could have avoided seeing each other. In any case, it is curious to point out that there are only three photographs of the Jesse couple and their son. All three were taken during my father's first trip to America in 1960. They were originally slides and, on account of that, I am sure that my mother was unaware of who figured in them because, otherwise, she would have disposed of them. Upon discovering the set of slides myself many years later after my mother's passing and viewing them, it was nothing short of a revelation for me. Eventually, I had a photographer convert the three slides where the Jesses figure into prints and added them to one of the family albums.

And, on that same letter Laura suggests something that is puzzling and yet true because it applies to some immigrants once they retire. She puts forward the idea that her old husband is thinking of retiring sometime in the future and of returning to his native São Miguel but that, on account of António's death, that idea has been put in the backburner for the time being. It's a mystery why, after living for so many years in America and having a son born in that country, he would want to return to a relatively poor part of the world. Perhaps because his American pension converted to *escudos* would guarantee a comfortable life in the island? He would not be the first immigrant to think along those lines with sometimes disastrous consequences for the unity of the family. The sons and daughters of most Azorean immigrants do not speak fluent Portuguese and, therefore, would find it extremely difficult to adapt to life in the Azores. They would feel like fishes out of the water trying to integrate into Azorean society.

On this subject, Dr. Laura Fernanda Bulger, who married a Canadian, John Bulger, and who lived in Toronto for a few years and taught Portuguese for a while at Harbord Collegiate Institute, an academic secondary school run by the Toronto District School Board, before moving on to teach the language at the University of Toronto, wrote an interesting book of short stories entitled *Vaivém* (*Back and Forth*). It tells the stories of some Portuguese families who, after living for many years in Canada, and once they have accumulated some wealth, decide to sell everything they own: home, furniture, cars, etc., and return with their offspring to their native country, in this case Portugal, thinking, erroneously, that their children will adapt easily to daily life there. Many of these families, after just a few months in Portugal, find themselves back in Canada to start all over again because their dream of a happy retirement in their native country turned sour almost upon arrival. The parents found it challenging to adapt to daily life in a country whose customs had evolved without them noticing it during their long absence. For their children, the new reality was even harsher to accept because, all of a sudden, they had been pulled out of school in Canada, where subjects are taught in English or French, and where they had established friendships, to be thrown into a school system totally different from the only one that they had ever known and where everything was taught in a language that they hardly knew, Portuguese. It was a recipe for disaster. All this brought about numerous disagreements and fights among family members which, in turn, brought the realization for the parents that if the unity and survival of the family was to prevail, they had to return to Canada. Woefully, such stories reflect a dream that had turned into a living nightmare for all concerned. Who would have thought that such a bizarre idea would have even crossed Aníbal's mind?

But what is even more puzzling is that Laura says that her old husband was not only thinking of returning in his old age to São Miguel, but that he was also thinking of renting the house that belonged to the Machado family and where Cristiano had lived for free after his marriage, if it were to be available at the time of his return. Life does indeed take all sorts of twists and turns!

In her last letter, written fairly close to the Christmas season of 1962, she mentions some of the gifts that my mother and I would be receiving from the Jesse family. She had found a certain Mr. Aristides de Sousa Travassos, a trustworthy acquaintance, to bring them to São Miguel. He would be sailing from Boston in an ocean liner named Saturnia (Vulcânia and Satúrnia, two Italian ships, stopped regularly in Ponta Delgada on their transatlantic voyages between Europe and North America and on the reverse trip in the 1950s and 1960s) with a scheduled stop in Ponta Delgada. Furthermore, in this city, the gentleman in question had an address fairly close to Virgínio's house. He would be doing Laura a favor by bringing a package for my mother and me. In it, there would be an overcoat, a raincoat, two items that belonged to her son who had outgrown them, a green wool sweater, a special Christmas gift from Laura for me, and some toys such as a cowboy revolver with its belt and holster, a box of building blocks, a deck of cards, and a water-based coloring set, all gifts courtesy of Val. For my mother, there would be a black suit consisting of a skirt and jacket. Regrettably, Laura claims that she had not had a chance to buy her some nylons as she had been sick with the flu.

So, that particular Christmas, I put on the green sweater, played with the building blocks and painted with the coloring set, all items that had the exotic smell of a foreign country, America. In Virgínio's home, however, no one played card games; the favorite game was dominoes. So, the deck of cards was put away for some future use. As far as the revolver with its accompanying belt and holster were concerned, I did not find much use for either one almost immediately afterwards because most of my friends no longer played cowboys and Indians. But the overcoat and the raincoat served me well that winter, and whenever I put them on someone would recognize the foreign smell that emanated from each one of those two articles of clothing and would ask me where I had gotten that stuff. With the passage of time, I stopped wearing them because I outgrew them myself. Sadly, but not surprisingly, not a single one of these gifts replaced in my life the permanent absence of my father. A void that would be there for the rest of my life.

After this last letter, all correspondence between Elzira and Laura, two women connected by fate and love for the same man, stopped altogether. There are no further traces of any letters between the two of them. The only plausible explanation for this outcome is that my mother had discovered by then my father's infidelity through the stash of letters found in his desk at the Governo Civil. In order to salvage her own self-esteem and pride, she saw no other alternative but to put a final stop to all communication with her rival whose collaboration was no longer needed anyways since all business transactions with the American companies had been finalized. In spite of her best attempts to cover up the love affair with António, Laura had been caught lying about it. For the rest of her living days, Elzira, for the rest of her living days, would regard the adulteress as the main protagonist in the tragic events that occurred at the Paramount Hotel in New York, events that transformed overnight her destiny and mine.

30

Virgínio Gets Mail from Laura Too

With respect to Laura's six letters addressed to Virgínio, they were more formal than the ones sent to Elzira and dealt mostly with António's export business and how to conclude the negotiations as quickly as possible in America. But, inevitably, some of them address other specific concerns such as his business associates, the return of his suitcase and personal items to Ponta Delgada by a trusted acquaintance, the infighting going on among the Machado family members, and the short film that had been shot at the funeral parlor and at the exit of Saint Anthony's church for the benefit of his immediate family in São Miguel since nobody could attend the funeral and pay their final respects to a man who had been so instrumental in their lives.

Regarding the business, she assures Virgínio that she is doing her utmost to move things along by phoning the Musolino Co. on a regular basis. She states, as she had already done several times in her correspondence with Elzira, that the firm is reputable and that, eventually, she will receive the money that is owed to her. She recommends patience.

Concerning António's business partners, she informs Virgínio that she does not trust Mr. João Miranda's intentions and cautions him and Elzira to keep their eyes open with respect to some undeserved settlement claim that could be coming from him.

Virgínio, as a chauffeur, taxi driver, knew a lot of people in São Miguel. So, whenever he found out that someone was visiting the US, especially the Boston area, he would ask the person if he could possibly bring back António's suitcase. Specifically, he had his hopes pinned on a certain Mr. Brigida who had relatives in Fall River. But for one reason or another, sadly, this chosen candidate and Laura never connected and the opportunity evaporated as the months passed. Eventually, through Mr. Mota, a connection at the PAA travel agency in Boston, a trustworthy woman was found, a certain Mrs. Silva, who was going to return by ship to São Miguel. Out of her kindness and goodwill, she accepted the responsibility of bringing António's suitcase to Ponta Delgada, at long last.

As for the personal disagreements separating the Machado family members, its source was the updating of the family house. Although António had come up with the money to initiate the renovations under the impression that his two brothers and sister would participate in the divvying up of the expenses, the reality was that they were not interested in spending their own money on the project. Besides, they felt threatened by his initiative. They were convinced that he was making improvements to the property with the ultimate intention of buying them out, and that did not appeal to them. Now that António was dead, they were hesitating in paying their fair share of the expenses. There was nothing that Elzira could do to coerce them to do the right thing, the ethical thing. The knives were out…

I also alluded elsewhere to the fact that Laura had firm ideas about certain family members. One of the individuals that she singles out in pejorative terms is José, the youngest of the Machado brothers, the one who took the initiative of kicking out of the Machado family abode my mother and me within two months of his brother passing away, and the same man who informed me of my father's death. She refers to him as being not only somewhat of a crazy man, but also a coward. On her letter to Virgínio, dated October 12th, 1961, she says:

> *Sr. Virgínio, fiquei ciente de tudo que me diz a respeito de tudo o que se passa por aí; parece impossível haver um desacordo destes entre a família que sempre estimei. É verdade que entre eles existia um, que não só era maluco como também cobarde, mas a restante família sempre a tive na mais alta consideração. Afinal, fico mesmo pateta com tudo isso, apesar de já ter conhecimento do que se passou com os concertos, contado por António. Mas a verdade é que se António fosse vivo tinha posto tudo direito.*

(Mr. Virgínio, I am aware of everything that you are telling me with regards to everything that is going on over there [Ponta Delgada]; it seems impossible that there is such a disagreement between the family members of a family that I always respected. It's true that among them there was one who was not only crazy but also a coward [José], but I always thought highly of the rest of the family. All in all, I am dumfounded with everything that is going on, even though I already knew everything concerning the renovations thanks to António. But the truth is that if António were alive, he would fix everything.)

On the topic of José's cowardice, it is of interest to point out that, whenever he saw at a distance my mother walking on a street in Ponta Delgada after his brother's death and after kicking her out of the Machado residence, he used to hide in the first shop in sight with an open door so that he would not have to face her which seems to corroborate what Laura is saying about the man even though she had no knowledge of this particular pattern of behavior on his part. Regrettably, however, she does not elaborate on the specific reasons why she labels him a coward. They would have shed some light on the particular nature of their relationship and, more importantly, what led her to consider him a weakling.

Finally, as far as the short film taken at the funeral parlor and at the exit from the church is concerned, when it finally came to the Azores, it ended up in Aida's hands who happened to be in the island of Santa

Maria at the time with her husband and children. Her husband, Henrique, had been posted momentarily to the town of Vila do Porto to serve as the chief operating officer at the local city hall. In Laura's letter dated March 26th, 1962, she expresses disappointment and outrage at the fact that we had not yet seen the film as we were the ones for whom it had been made in the first place. Elzira only received the package containing it on June 25th, three months later. The explanation for the delay in sending it to her was simple: the other family members wanted to see the contents of the morbid film before Elzira and me. It was an act of pure selfishness on their part. At long last, when Aida did send it to Ponta Delgada, it did not come straight to Elzira's hands; instead, the small package was addressed to Virgínio. Result? Others got to view it before the most important ones themselves had a chance to do so. Speaking of adding insult to injury!

In Laura's letter dated February 21st, 1962, one item in particular that caught my attention was the following: she expresses surprise at not receiving any news from Elzira as of late. She goes on to confess that, as far as she was aware, she had not offended her in any way shape of form and that, therefore, she did not understand the cause for the lack of news from her. She would like Virgínio to shine some light on this mystery. The possible explanation for Elzira's silence is that, at some point before or after Christmas of 1961, she found out about her husband's love affair with Laura. If before she had had only strong suspicions about it, now she possessed concrete evidence of the illicit relationship in her own hands. There could not be any more doubts in her mind. Needless to say, she was devastated by this news and, at the same time, furious about it. So, she stopped writing to her until she cooled down and realized that she still needed her rival, whether she liked it or not, in order to conclude satisfactorily what António had not been able to finish in America.

Another detail of interest, one that is also present in Laura's first letters to Elzira, is the precision with which she describes an event. A case in point is the arrival of António's remains in Boston from

New York. In her second letter dated August 31st, 1961, the day after António's funeral, she states that the body arrived at seven thirty-five in the evening of August 26th and that shortly afterwards, at nine o'clock sharp, she finally received the Power of Attorney from Ponta Delgada. She seems to be in a most impressionable state of mind, one that makes her highly aware of all the circumstances surrounding the events of the recent tragedy as they evolve. She also confesses, as I previously pointed out, being on the verge of a nervous breakdown as a direct result of her involvement in the tragedy and the added pressure of being the sole eyewitness of the events as they unfolded.

Like Elzira's copies of the letters to Laura, none of Virgínio's to her were kept. In other words, there were no rough copies left behind for one to consult. This is, of course, normal since very few people keep handwritten copies of their own correspondence. Therefore, one has to resort to one's imagination in order to figure out what exactly was being discussed in them. That said, the content of Laura's letters to Virgínio, just like the content of hers to Elzira, fill the missing gaps and tell a compelling story by using a narrative that is poignant, pathetic and almost believable if it were not for the contradictions of the facts here and there.

So, the question is: what to make of this woman named Laura? On one hand, she was perceived by Elzira, and the rest of the women in her family, as the adulteress, a woman who had deliberately seduced a responsible married man and a caring father. For them, she was nothing short of a whore who had destroyed a happy family. She was also directly blamed for his death although no one had proof of her direct involvement in it except to say that he had died in her arms and in her room at the Paramount Hotel. Nevertheless, that alone was enough for them to blame her for it. For all of them, she was as guilty as sin. As far as they were concerned, António himself was left off the hook, absolved of any culpability in the affair as if he had not played a significant role in it, too. The cache of love letters found in his desk at work eventually made Elzira realize that he was not an innocent bystander after all. It's also curious that the only people in Elzira's family who raised suspicions about Aníbal's involvement in António's demise were the men. They thought that a jilted and dishonored old man, a cuckold, would seek retribution for the affront. But their opinion on the matter was outnumbered by that of the women and, somehow, he was left mostly unscathed by the ordeal although, come to think of it, it's difficult to understand how a much older man than António, he was seventy-one at the time, would have taken kindly seeing his thirty-five-year-old wife take off to New York with a forty-three-year-old Dom Juan. What did he think they were going to do by staying overnight in that city? Just take care of business? That would have been unrealistic and highly unlikely. Given the old man's socio-economic and cultural background, one has to assume that his heart would be set on revenge at any cost on account of his wife's treachery.

It's relevant to note in this regard that when the old barber died in 1975, at the age of eighty-five, he was not buried in the plot where António's remains lie in the Cambridge Cemetery. No, instead Aníbal was put to rest in the plot next to it. In fact, to this day, the only two people buried in António's grave remain himself and Laura who died much later, on November 21st, 2001. The two reunited for eternity in death. Was she saving since 1961 a spot for herself in António's plot? Why wouldn't she want to be buried with her own husband, the man who had brought her to the "Promised Land"? It's a decision that defies logic unless there was a very good reason for it which, of course, we won't ever know. Life is full of mysteries.

31

A Business Loss

For someone with only a superficial knowledge of her husband's business dealings and handicapped by a basic education, the entire affair of his untimely death must have been a nightmarish experience for Elzira. In the end, according to her detailed notes, a total of 82 bags of fava beans weighing 50 kilos each vanished into thin air for a loss of $1,076.00 USD. Furthermore, out of another batch of 355 bags, of which 325 were unpeeled and 20 peeled, left on consignment with the Musolino Co., there was a net loss of $855.79 USD. After converting the total losses into Portuguese *escudos*, at an average rate of exchange of 28$52 *escudos* per dollar, the amount came to a staggering 55 094$65 *escudos*. A small fortune in 1963. The poor woman must have felt that the world was caving in on her and that her husband's adventures in the world of private enterprise had been nothing short of a disaster.

So, according to Elzira, who carefully kept track of all the money associated with António's business adventures, or perhaps one should call them misadventures in America, from the moment of his death until they were concluded, the balance was nothing short of a major setback and, as a consequence, a source of great disappointment and stress for her. She was left utterly confused by the unforeseen turn of events. How could 82 bags of fava beans have disappeared mysteriously from the port of Ponta Delgada at the moment of being loaded into the ship? And how could another 10 bags have vanished in similar circumstances from the port of New York? Also, how could there be a loss of $855,79 USD associated with the consignment sale of the 325 bags of unpeeled fava beans and the 20 bags of peeled ones that were left in the hands of the Musolino Co., a company of which António thought so highly? And, finally, on top of all these losses, there were the expenses associated with the credit line opened by her husband at the Banco Português do Atlântico, in Ponta Delgada, which amounted to another 12 154$70 *escudos*. When all was said and done, the export business had lost a grand total of 63 687$77 *escudos*. If one takes this figure and subtracts it from what she actually received from the sale of all the fava beans, the margin of profit was very modest indeed. In other words, António's efforts had not been worth the trouble, certainly not in 1961. All his *frenesí* had translated into very little financial gain. On this point, Laura, in her last letter to Elzira, dated November 22nd, 1962, many months after his death, concludes:

> *É mesmo de lamentar tudo isso, pois foi uma grande perca que tiveste em tudo. Peço a Deus para que lá em casa te paguem os concertos que António fez e o dinheiro que ele tinha emprestado à Aida, porque calculo que isto já te ajudava bastante.*

> (It's to lament all that, because it was a great loss that you had in everything. I pray to God that people at home will pay you for the renovations that António undertook and the money that he had lent Aida, because I imagine that this would help you a lot.)

There was no better way to put it. She accurately summarizes Elzira's financial losses without knowing that there was still more to the story.

To complicate Elzira's financial situation, the life insurance policy of 500 000$00 *escudos* that António had signed for with the Companhia Europeia did not pay a cent upon his death, possibly because he had perished outside of Portugal although that would have been the major reason for him to have acquired insurance in the first place; and another policy of 75 000$00 *escudos* with the Cofre de Previdência da Junta Geral, a group insurance plan for government employees which was run by the Ministry of Finances and towards which António had contributed to ever since 1946, only paid the sum of 32 500$00 to his widow in 1962. As a side note, it is worthwhile to remark that in 1974 I received the sum of 20 719$00 *escudos* from the Cofre de Previdência, my share of the pie, which converted to Canadian dollars amounted to $803,63. It was a decent sum of money for an undergraduate university student at the University of Toronto, such as myself, at the time who would have to work full time an entire summer in order to put that amount of cash aside to pay tuition in the fall. So, altogether the Cofre de Previdência paid out a total of 52 679$60 *escudos*. Again, one is surprised to find out that António was under the impression that he was entitled to receive at least 75 000$00 *escudos* when, in reality, he could only get much less if he had read attentively the insurance policy. The moral of the story is that many good folks buy insurance policies thinking that they are getting something when, in fact, they are getting something else. The devil is in the details, the small print. Most people's expectations are never quite met when it comes to collecting any money from insurance companies. Why is it that most insurance plans never seem to bring financial relief to those who need it when they need it the most? Something to ponder about if one is seriously thinking of purchasing insurance to safeguard the future of loved ones.

The icing on the cake, ironically speaking, turned out to be the added cost connected with António's burial in the US. The Joseph A. Costa Sons Memorial Funeral Home charged $900.36 USD for it and, according to Laura, the price tag did not include the purchase of the cemetery plot because the Jesses already owned it. According to Jessica Mitford who wrote an informative book published in 1963 entitled *The America Way of Death*, the average cost of a funeral service and burial in 1961 would have been around $750.00 USD. If that was the case, it's difficult to understand what kind of a deal the Jesse's friend at the funeral home came up with to save my mother some money. Regardless, the $900.36 converted to Portuguese *escudos* at the time, at the rate of 28$52 per dollar, amounted to 25 678$26. When one considers that António's annual salary as a civil servant in 1961 was a mere 6 000$00 *escudos*, it represented a fair sum of money. And, to add insult to injury, his remains were interred in a cemetery so far away from Ponta Delgada that nobody from his immediate family would be able to travel there any time soon to pay their final respects. Symbolically, the funeral bill put a financial exclamation mark at the very end of António's short life and even shorter personal business adventures in the "land of opportunity".

By contrast, Virgínio's total burial costs in Toronto, Canada, on September 5th, 1973, organized by the Turner & Porter Funeral Directors Limited, at their Roncesvalles Chapel, were $1,010.00 CAD, plot included, twelve years after António's funeral. Taking into account the inflation rate and the fact that the Canadian dollar was worth less than the American one in relation to the Portuguese *escudo*, one cannot escape the inevitable conclusion that the amount charged by the Joseph A. Costa Sons Memorial Funeral Home back in 1961 was not a bargain at all by any stretch of the imagination.

As for Elzira's own funeral costs on November 25th, 1981, in Ponta Delgada, taken care of by the Agência Funerária Silva, they came to 81 331$00 *escudos*. The poor woman died while on a visit to São Miguel in order to attend a family wedding. It seems that my parents do have a preference for passing away during trips abroad and as far away from me as possible. In the case of Elzira's funeral, however, I did have a chance to pay my last respects to my dear mother and attend her funeral in the company of my wife who was there to lend moral support at a very difficult time in my life.

32

The Challenging 1960s in Ponta Delgada

Let's review the facts that made the decade of 1960 so challenging for Elzira and, indirectly, for me as well. On August 23rd, 1961, there was a flurry of telegrams going back and forth between Ponta Delgada and Boston and New York. Before António's body could be released form the New York City morgue, a Power of Attorney had to be sent by Elzira to Laura enabling her to make decisions in her stead regarding António's remains and personal items.

A couple of days later, thanks to the direct intervention of the Consulate General of Portugal in New York and its lawyer, Dr. Jerome Teich, the release of the body occurred on August 25th. The Consul and Dr. Teich, against all odds, had been successful in pulling some strings with the local city officials for this to happen without the Power of Attorney on hand. Also, on the same date, and because of the two gentlemen, the NYPD released António's personal items, which had been collected from the Paramount Hotel on August 22nd, to the consulate. These, however, had to be safeguarded at the chancery until the Consul General got the Power of Attorney from Elzira authorizing Laura to take possession of them. The following day, on August 26th, António's remains were promptly sent to Boston by train where, upon arrival, a funeral representative from the Costa Funeral Home took possession of them.

That very same evening of August 26th, Laura finally received Elzira's much anticipated Power of Attorney and forwarded immediately a photocopy to the Consulate General of Portugal in New York. It was an essential formality for the release of António's personal items which were eventually delivered to her in person by someone from the Chancery while on a personal trip to Boston.

In the intervening days, since the cost of sending António's cadaver to Ponta Delgada or of burying it in New York would have been prohibitive, the decision had been made, with Elzira's consent, to inter his remains at the Cambridge Cemetery where the Jesse family owned a plot. The widow would be, thus, saving some money which was in short supply. Besides, this decision would enable António's friends and acquaintances in and around Boston to pay their final respects to him.

While these decisions were being made, the Costa Funeral Home was busy planning the wake and the interment. The former took place on August 28th and 29th and the latter on August 30th. It was an ordeal for all concerned. However, for Elzira and me there had not been any closure as all of these events took place far away from us, that is to say in another country with different ways and customs of dealing with someone's death. It took some time before reality sank for both my mother and me and for us to accept the reality that we would never see again António again. As for the film that was shot at the funeral parlor, it was only viewed once in 1962; it brought back horrible memories and the dark days that followed the dreadful event. Although the intention of whoever shot it may have been good and even honorable, given that the immediate family of the deceased lived so far away and could not attend his wake and funeral, the feelings that its viewing produced in my mother and I were awful, for no normal human being enjoys seeing in film, to be played and replayed forever, a husband and a father lying motionless inside a coffin.

The next few months were extremely stressful, nerve-racking and chaotic for Elzira. Totally unprepared to deal with the unfinished business affairs left by her husband, she had to rely on her father for support along the way, a man who had mistreated all his four children when they were growing up. As I pointed out before, physical and emotional abuse were common currency in the Faria family home. And when Elzira felt most vulnerable and needed the most help, her father never missed a chance to put her down, resentful of the fact that she had had a wonderful life while married to António.

In order to wrap up António's export business, numerous letters were written back and forth between Elzira and Laura, and Elzira and the Musolino Co. during the next months. His business partners had to be compensated for their collaboration and investment in the enterprise, and the banks that had offered António business loans had to be repaid. So, between August 22nd, 1961, and November 22nd, 1962, the topic of conversation in the evenings between daughter and father was essentially limited to figuring out how to extract from the Musolino Co. the amount of money owed António from the sale of the rest of the fava beans left on consignment. It goes without saying that the company, once António was out of the picture, felt in no hurry to settle the account with the widow any time soon and she, consequently, could not just turn around and repay the bank loans, his business partners, and even the balance of the unpaid funeral bill. The situation left much to be desired and for days on end the poor widow upon waking up in the morning had very little to look forward to throughout the day. The thought that she was now my sole provider, supporter and defender kept her engaged in the battle for survival.

But, aside from having to settle the accounts with the American companies and António's Azorean associates, she also had to get used to being a widow in a small city where widows were generally looked down upon and, consequently, not respected because most of them were perceived as being poor and dependent. Life was not going to be rosy for Elzira in the future. Nevertheless, in spite of all adversity, she found the inner strength to carry on and defend my interests to the best of her abilities. People do have a tendency to find the willpower, the courage and sheer determination to rise to the occasion and face enormous personal challenges when cornered by life's unforeseen blows. With the passage of time, she eventually accepted her fate and saw to it that I completed elementary school and that I was enrolled in high school. António's wishes were slowly but surely materializing themselves in spite of his absence. In the process, however, Elzira sacrificed herself so that I lacked nothing. The least that can be said about her is that she was a kind, loving, unselfish, and most generous soul.

In short, the 1960s were in stark contrast with the 1950s for my mother and me. I am tempted to say, when I think about her life, that her happiest moments were in the late 1940s and throughout the 1950s. She had married the man she loved and bore him a son who became her pride and joy. Thanks to António, she had enjoyed a carefree lifestyle for fourteen years. And, although the 1960s started with a wonderful month-long trip to Continental Portugal and Madeira, a trip that she would remember forever with fondness, the decade quickly turned to grief with the unexpected passing of her husband in August of 1961. Suddenly, she saw herself in a most vulnerable position as the sole breadwinner, protector and defender of her young son who, going forward, would not benefit from the support of a caring father and mentor as he grew up. As the 1960s passed slowly and as the age of mandatory military service approached for me, she started contemplating another scenario, emigrating to Canada where her sister Eduarda and her younger brother João had established themselves, to save me from conscription and, possibly, being killed in Africa where a raging guerilla war was evolving in the old Portuguese colonies. If this scenario came to be, she would be facing different uncertainties than the ones that she had become used to in Ponta Delgada because she would be living in a country whose two official languages she did not understand and, most importantly, where she would have to find work, without a trade and much less a profession, in order for the two of us to make ends meet.

But she was the type of mother who would do anything and everything in her power to keep me safe for as long as she could. She was a courageous and brave woman. But if the plan to emigrate to Canada came to be, the 1970s promised to be a definite challenge for the two of us.

33

Roberto's School Friends Save the Decade

As far as I was concerned, daily life just kept happening except for the fact that my father had suddenly disappeared from my presence leaving a vacuum which was not filled by my maternal grandfather. Luckily for me, I made friends easily in both elementary and high school and spent more and more of my free time in their company throughout the 1960s.

Ponta Delgada was a relatively small city in those days and, therefore, all the young boys who had started elementary school in grade one at the age of seven in my part of town knew one another quite well by the time they finished their studies in grade four and moved on to high school. We had spent, after all, four years together, and with the same teacher, an older, non-nonsense woman whom all students respected and addressed as Dona Mariana Carreiro. Only at the age of eleven, when a choice had to be made between going on to the *liceu*, an academic high school, or to the *escola industrial*, a trade high school, did some of the boys go separate ways and, inevitably, as the years passed, lost contact with one another.

So, after passing the examinations at the end of the four years of elementary school, I enrolled in the only academic institution in Ponta Delgada: the then Liceu Nacional de Ponta Delgada, today Liceu

Antero de Quental, named after the most influential of the local poets and one of the greatest national intellectuals of the XIX century. The high school occupied the former Palácio de Fonte Bela, built in the XVII century and transformed into a high school in 1921. To get there, I walked westward along Rua da Pranchinha which turned into Rua da Boa Nova, passing in front of the house where I was born and had lived until the age of nine, then I followed along Rua Engenheiro José Cordeiro, Rua do Perú, Rua do Mercado, Rua de São João, Rua Machado dos Santos and, at the corner of Rua do Brum, I turned right and there, just north of the garden called Mártires da Pátria, stood the yellow and white high school building. It was a walk that took a good thirty minutes or so. During inclement weather this daily routine was somewhat disrupted and instead of walking I would take the *urbana*, a small bus that did the runs within the city, to get to my classes. At the Liceu Nacional, aside from keeping some of my closest friends from elementary school who were enrolled there, I made some fresh new ones who proved to be invaluable to me in my early, middle and late adolescence.

After my father's death, as time slowly moved on and when I was alone, I felt generally restless and bored to tears and tried to keep myself busy by biking in my immediate neighborhood when the weather was good, kite flying in the summer time in the backyard that fronted the ocean, reading comic books, and by going to Cinema Marítimo on Sunday afternoons. Later on, as a teenager, in the winter, on Saturday afternoons or evenings I would go to the movies at Teatro Micaelense, and to the beach every day in the summer. These were activities that I did always in the company of my friends. In particular, the last one was always fun because it involved hitchhiking to Praia do Pópulo, in São Roque, a distance of a mere six kilometers from Ponta Delgada. That's what boys did in pairs in the morning of those careless dog days of summer. No one in São Miguel thought that hitchhiking was a dangerous activity; it was simply the cheapest way to get to the beach if one could find a willing and generous driver who happened to be on his way to Lagoa, a small town to the east of São Roque, or elsewhere, along the south side of the island.

In the Ponta Delgada of the 1960s, high school students did not work part-time during vacation time. So, all young people had a lot of free time at their disposal. Nevertheless, a lot of this free time was not wasted in vain. Instead, groups of friends used to get together in the afternoon at some favorite *café*, such as O Gil, a favorite hangout for teenagers, for an espresso and to discuss all sorts of current issues. It was there that a lot of opinions and ideas were put forth and discussed at nauseum. Some of these shaped our actions as young teenagers and made us commit to social justice causes and political reform in a part of Portugal, the Azores, that a lot of us considered to be out of step with the rest of the world.

My favorite partner in elementary school was Marco António. His father, Mr. Moura, worked for Radio Marconi and he liked to speak French with the two of us when we started high school (French was the first foreign language to be introduced in those days as part of the high school curriculum). Going to Marco António's home on Saturday afternoons was fun because, after homework was done, we would go down to the backyard and shoot around a soccer ball to get rid of some excess energy. I remember the Moura family for another reason: Marco António's dad was the proud owner of a brand-new pale green Fiat 500 and, on occasion, he would give his son and friends a ride to school. To this day, I still recall the unique smell inside the cabin of that brand-new car. In the winter time, Mr. Moura also used to put on driving gloves, a characteristic that always struck me as unusual because he was the only man that I knew at the time who had that rare habit in Ponta Delgada, a city that never gets really cold in the winter.

Next to Marco António, stood Emanuel. The Vasconcelos', his parents, had a summer home nestled amid several *estufas de ananases*, pineapple greenhouses, in Fajã de Baixo, a town located a short distance to the north of Ponta Delgada. Every once in a while, during the long summer vacation, I was invited to spend the day there and that was always a lot of fun because both of us would build kites from scratch and then try to fly them in a setting where there was almost never any sea breeze, a fact that made kite flying almost an impossibility, but one that did not discourage us from attempting to fly our brand-new kites for hours. Emanuel had been a late arrival for the Vasconcelos. He had a much older brother who was a university student in the field of mathematics at the Universidade de Coimbra. As most Azorean university students studying in mainland Portugal in those days (there was no university in the Azores until the mid-seventies), he used to return to São Miguel on vacation in the summer. At the time, he was dating a beautiful young woman who, when I was in grade one, had been a teacher candidate in Dona Mariana Carreiro's class, my elementary school teacher. When she saw me for the first time at the summer house, a couple of years later, she still remembered teaching me and asked if I, in turn, still remembered her. Out of shyness and cowardice I, blushing, said that I did not, although I did remember her vividly on account of her beauty and kindness towards me in that grade one class. After this blatant, unexpected, and totally unnecessary lie, I felt terrible about it and regretted having been such an idiot by not telling her the truth. She deserved better than that because she was such a caring person and would have loved to know that she had made a lasting impression in my young mind. I have lived the rest of my life with guilt feelings about that idiotic lie.

Moving on to high school, my best friend became Luís whom I called França because it was part of his family name, and because it sounded out of the ordinary. Nobody else that I knew had a last name like that. Although we were attending different high schools, our friendship flourished and, for a few years the two of us became inseparable, especially when we got girlfriends who were also neighbors and friends. Luís went on to become an important visual artist in Portugal.

Another friend was Zé, a nickname for José, whom I called Cabral, again because it was part of his family name. He was the son of a medical doctor and, in the summer of 1968, he invited me to accompany him to the island of São Jorge where his father's sister lived with her husband. They were a childless older couple. It turned out to be a wonderful vacation because Zé's aunt and her husband were incredible hosts who made it their duty to show off their island from one point to the other. The island of São Jorge is, as everyone knows, famous for the cheese that bears the same name and that is appreciated all over the world by cheese connoisseurs. Also, São Jorge is only a mere 20km north of Pico, its closest neighbor in the Azores so-called Central Group of islands, called thus because its main feature, Montanha do Pico, is the highest mountain in Portugal at 2,351m or 7, 708ft. It was simply amazing to wake up every morning and admire that majestic mountain such a short distance away whose summit on many days was above the clouds.

Still, another friend was Necas, the short form for Nectário, the son of an optometrist, and yet another one was Tó, a nickname for António, the son of a pilot working for SATA, the Azorean Airliner, who just happened to be piloting the twin-engine Hawker Siddeley HS 748 manufactured by Avro, a British company, the day that my mother and I left Ponta Delgada to Santa Maria to board there a CP (Canadian Pacific) airplane that would take us to Toronto, Canada. I have not forgotten the kind gesture displayed by Tó's father for asking one of the flight attendants to bring me to the cockpit so that I would see the island of Santa Maria emerge from the sea on that beautiful sunny morning of December 22nd, 1969. It was an unforgettable experience. I was saddened to find out a few years later that Tó had committed suicide over a love relationship gone sour. And there were others, too many to be mentioned here. All of them were excellent company and kept me interested and engaged in all sorts of activities and issues.

In short, in one way or another, we were all committed to political, social and educational reforms in a Portugal still dominated in the late 1960s by a fascist government, that of António Salazar, which forbade and punished severely any political dissention. The Salazar years were certainly a very dark period in Portuguese politics which caused massive emigration from a country where so many of its citizens still remained illiterate and poor in the middle of the XX century and saw no future to better themselves if they were to stay put, especially in a relatively poor area like the Azores where professional opportunities for so many people were non-existent.

Needless to say, these friendships came to an abrupt end when I emigrated to Canada in 1969 at the age of seventeen. When someone emigrates, it's like a premature death of that individual for all those left behind. In the space of just a few seconds one disappears from the daily life of relatives, friends and acquaintances alike. Time marches on for everyone and, inevitably, all concerned get used to a new reality. Most relationships do not survive sudden physical separations that go on for years.

So, for a while there were still a few letters written back and forth between myself and my friends but, with time, those slowly became more and more infrequent and, eventually, stopped altogether. I was busy in my new country, a country which I loved from the very beginning, and so were my friends back home many of whom had left in turn São Miguel to pursue higher education in mainland Portugal. *C'est la vie*!

I had a chance, between 1969 and 2018, to get together in Ponta Delgada with only two of my former close friends: França, in 1987, and Cabral, in 2018, who happened to be there on vacation at the same time that I was there on vacation myself. Two chance encounters. Both occasions provided a unique opportunity to touch base after so many years had gone by, and to take stock of what everyone had done in the intervening time. As pointed out before, the former had become an arts instructor and the latter a surgeon. Both lived in Continental Portugal and only returned occasionally to São Miguel. It was during these two brief encounters that I realized how many of my former friends had actually left the island, for one reason or another, to establish new roots elsewhere.

Still, in spite of being busy with my friends and school, occasionally the memory of my father would pop into my head. Sometimes António's name would come up in conversations with relatives or family friends and acquaintances who remembered the man that he had been with fondness, affection and *saudade*, longing. Nobody spoke about him in pejorative terms. On the contrary, they took advantage of the opportunity to highlight his many attributes in my presence. On other occasions, his memory would be evoked because I would come across some of his personal items that my mother was so carefully safekeeping and that were destined for my own use as an adult. These flash-backs brought about mostly sad feelings on my part because they reminded me of the fact that the man who had loved me so dearly, my father, was gone forever and that the material objects that had been part and parcel of his daily life could never replace his existence. But what I regretted the most was the impossibility of having a conversation with him as an adult, a friendly man-to-man chat with the person who had partnered with a woman, my mother, to give me the gift of life. The realization that I would never be able to have a true measure of what António had been like made me melancholy and tearful. However, ever since the day that I had been told that *um homem não chora*, a man does not cry, I refrained from shedding a tear or two publicly. As the days, months and years came and went, one day I was shocked to realize that I could not remember any longer the sound of my father's voice. His memory was quickly fading into thin air.

In conclusion, if it had not been for my indispensable friends, life would not have been very pleasant. Their friendship and camaraderie literally saved the 1960s for me and the least that can be said about it is that I was very sorry to leave them behind when I emigrated to Canada. The last time that I saw all of them together was on that December morning, in 1969, when they came to the airport to say good-bye to a friend who was going to disappear from their daily lives, perhaps forever, and who was travelling to the end of the Earth, so it seemed to them and to me, too. It was a bittersweet moment for all concerned, especially for me who was henceforth going to face life in Canada as a teenager without any friends and with a very limited knowledge of English. I had many apprehensions about what lay ahead and whether

I had it in me what it took to succeed in a foreign country. For me, at that specific moment in time, only one thing was for certain, it was not going to be easy.

34

In late 1975 Somerville, Massachusetts

I am sure that between August 22nd, 1961, the day António died, and December 1st, 1975, the day that Aníbal passed away, a period of fourteen years, the Jesses spoke numerous times at first and, as time passed and the memory of the episode started to fade, less and less frequently about what transpired in New York City and its aftermath and how it affected their personal lives. The disastrous event must have marked and changed forever the nature of their relationship as husband and wife. At the time of his death, he was eighty-five years old and Laura had just turned forty-nine. He was old enough to have been her grandfather. What could they still possibly have in common? Not much, I daresay.

It's fascinating to speculate about the content of the conversations that may, or may not, have occurred between them. Whenever the topic of António came up, for instance, who initiated the conversation? Him or her? And for what purpose? Were there mutual accusations of wrong doing? In other words, what was the nature and tone of their discussion? Did António's death in particular ever come up? Did Laura ever suspect her husband of having played some role in António's demise out of jealousy and hate for the Azorean rival? And if so, did she fear for her own safety?

Irrespective of the above considerations, I am sure that the old husband had observed carefully during the Labor Day weekend of 1960, when António had been invited by Laura for lunch at their home and stayed for dinner, too, how she interacted with him and he must have sensed right then and there that what connected these two individuals was definitely more than a simple friendship dating back to their youth in Ponta Delgada. Consequently, did he not perceive immediately António as a real threat to the stability of his relationship with his wife and, consequently, to his psychological wellbeing? Also, throughout 1960 and 1961, Aníbal must have suspected his wife of being actively planning something "special" for when António would return to Boston in the summer of 1961. I put forth elsewhere the possibility that he had discovered the secret correspondence between his wife and António during the winter of 1961 and of being psychologically distraught by it. He felt betrayed by her. So much so that he got physically sick and could not work for four months. Given his psychological profile, what puzzles me the most is why he would agree for the *micaelense* to stay at his house. Did he have a choice in the matter? Did Laura give him an ultimatum that he could not refuse? Was he afraid of the consequences if he did not accept willingly her wishes? In other words, did the possibility that she might leave him ever cross his mind? Did he accept her terms voluntarily or, on the other hand, only to cater to the whim of a woman who was so much younger than himself? All these considerations bring me to this question: who was the dominant force in the Jesse household from day to day?

Or, conversely, had António in 1960 promised to help them out financially when Laura offered her services as a translator of his business letters? He was the kind of man who would have offered to help, especially after finding out that at the age of seventy the barber surely was not in a position to continue to work for much longer. If he were to retire, the couple and their son would have to live on his government pension alone because Laura was unemployed; however, if Laura were to be financially compensated by António, their financial situation would stabilize. And if the Jesses had ambitions for their son to attend one day university, they would require money to finance his education, an expensive proposition in most countries, especially in America. In 1961, money did not seem to be abundant in the Jesse household.

What is known for sure is that Laura forced her poor husband to accept as inevitable the fact that António was going to stay at their house as a guest in the late summer of 1961 whether he liked the idea or not without revealing to him that she also planned to go with the Azorean Casanova to New York and stay there overnight in a hotel. Behind his back, she had planned, with some help from António, everything, which proves that she could be a manipulative and cunning woman when driven by a personal objective and, by the looks of it, that was the case.

At the time of his death, Aníbal was eighty-five years old and Laura had just turned forty-nine. He was old enough to be her grandfather. What could they still possibly have in common? Not much, I daresay.

It remains a mystery the kind of life that Laura led after becoming a widow, that is to say from 1975 until her own death in 2001. For instance, did she ever work for a living to make ends meet? Did she remarry? Did her health status, especially her nervous condition, improve with time? What became of her son Val? What did he make of himself? Was he, perhaps, drafted and sent to Vietnam? And if so, did he survive his tour of duty in that brutal war? I am sure that he would be in a position to shed light on several issues raised in this book if he were to be still alive but, thus far, all my attempts to locate him have been in vain.

To sum up, we have seen throughout the centuries that ordinary people are capable of anything and everything including, of course, cold-blooded murder if it is perceived as the only solution to restore their good name and honor. Indeed, many crimes of passion have been committed in the name of love or hate by people who, at first glance, looked perfectly normal and inoffensive but who, regrettably, proved to be quite the opposite, people capable of participating in atrocities of the worst kind. Whether on not António was the victim of such an attempt, we will never know for sure.

35

A Fresh Start for Elzira and Roberto in Toronto, Canada

My mother and I emigrated to Canada on December 22nd, 1969, thanks to the generosity of her youngest brother, João, who happened to have been all along my favorite uncle. He sponsored the two of us and saw to it that we got settled in our new country. Thanks to his friendship, kindness and generosity, I escaped being drafted into the Portuguese army and, perhaps, being sent to Africa where, alas, a few of my former friends from high school days in Ponta Delgada perished during the colonial guerrilla wars there.

Life in Toronto was not easy at first. It never seems to be for the vast majority of immigrants in spite of how well prepared they might think they are upon arriving at their new destination. Although English was part of the high school program in Portugal, my knowledge of the language left a lot to be desired. Fortunately, I was totally immersed in the language in my new high school in Toronto and, after a couple of years, I could speak it fluently. I completed my secondary studies at Bloor Collegiate Institute and, then, registered at the University of Toronto, St. Michael's College, one of the founding colleges of that university, graduating four years later with a bachelor's degree. Immediately afterwards, I enrolled in the Faculty of Education at the same university in order to obtain the necessary certification to become a high school teacher of French and Spanish. After that, the rest is history, so to speak. For me, Canada was indeed the "land of opportunity" for it afforded me a wonderful life at both the professional and personal levels. Even though I spent my formative years in São Miguel and that small island on the surface of the Earth continues to have a huge magnetic pull for me, nowadays I consider myself more Canadian than Azorean. Had I stayed in São Miguel, I would have been a very different person from the one that inhabits my skin today. There is no doubt about it. If nothing else, because human beings are a product of their economic, social and cultural environment and the people who are part and parcel of their daily life wherever they happen to live. There is no escaping this inevitable reality.

Looking back at all the events that unfolded in 1960 and 1961, I realize that I would have liked meeting personally this woman named Laura who played such a central and pivotal role during the last days of my father's life. That said, although I visited Somerville on many different occasions over the years on account of having married, in 1978, a beautiful woman of Azorean background whose parents had emigrated from Ponta Delgada to the US in 1967 and who had put roots in that city, I never looked her up. Before my own mother's death, in 1981, the thought of meeting Laura in person would have been inconceivable because it would have caused her a lot of emotional grief and distress; she would have perceived it as a betrayal by me, the son she had cared for and protected from the day I was born in 1952 and for whom she had devoted her entire life since my father's passing in 1961.

But there was nothing between 1981 and 2001 to stop me from having met personally Laura. My only excuse is that I was too busy living my own life and, quite frankly, not in the mood to look for someone associated with such a dark period in my own childhood and adolescence. Also, after the birth of my own daughter, in 1989, my priorities changed dramatically and she became the central focus of my life. It was only after retiring in 2017, truth be told, that I finally went back to the documentation left behind by my mother which, in the meantime, I had stored neatly away in a box for future consideration, that I thought seriously of writing my father's story. One has to be fortunate enough to live a long life in order to do something that should have been done long ago but that it was continually postponed for one reason or another. Starting in 2018, with much free time at my disposal now that I was fully retired, and on account of the pandemic, COVID-19, beginning in 2020, with all its personal restrictions of movement put in place by all levels of governments, the time seemed right to study the documentation and, hopefully, draw some conclusions from it in view of weaving a story based on it.

Time, it is said, is a great healer. I, eventually, got used to living without a father figure. On the other hand, my mother never recovered fully from the loss of the man of her dreams, one that had given her such a good life for fourteen years and a lovely son. From the moment she became a widow, she basically only lived to defend my interests and to make sure that my father's wish that I would one day be the proud recipient of a university degree became a reality. Not an easy task for a widow of thirty-seven who was left without too many financial resources at her disposal. The lack of money forced her to make countless personal sacrifices, which she never perceived as such given the type of person she was, that is to say extremely kind and generous. On top of that, she felt morally obligated to carry out her husband's final wishes. Consequently, she behaved in a most unselfish way, and her commitment to the cause, so to speak, never wavered. For that, I am eternally grateful to her.

After 1981, in each and every trip to São Miguel, I have made it a point of visiting the plot in the Cemitério de São Joaquim, the municipal cemetery in Ponta Delgada, where she and her own mother are buried and in 2022, my most recent trip to the Boston area, I visited once again the Cambridge Cemetery and was told, by the administrator at its office that, to this day, there are only two people buried in the plot where my father rests: himself and Laura. The grave's marker, however, only mentions her name.

In conclusion, António was indeed right about education being one of the keys to personal and professional satisfaction, happiness, and some degree of financial independence. He knew from personal experience that it would open professionally all sorts of doors for me that would otherwise stay permanently shut. When everything is said and done, education enables one to think critically and rationally about the society of which one is an integral part, and it allows one to figure out the role that one can and must play to make a positive difference for the betterment of present and future generations, and the health of the planet that we call Earth.

As a result of my father's vision, professionally, I was fortunate enough to become a high school teacher of French, Portuguese and Spanish in Canada for thirty-two years, including serving as Department head of Modern Languages for thirteen of those years in two different academic high schools. And, after retiring from the Toronto District School Board and while pursuing a Ph.D. degree in Québec literature at the University of Toronto, for the opportunity to be an instructor of French for the next seven years. As an educator, I enjoyed the privilege given to all teachers: that of bringing up and discussing with my students many relevant social justice issues, political causes, and environmental concerns by using the most powerful platform at my disposal, a classroom setting. My classes were filled with attentive, energetic and idealistic students eager to learn and get involved. To the best of my abilities, I did what I could to develop in them critical thinking skills so that they would become free thinkers, capable of making up their own minds on all sorts of issues by relying on facts rather than blatant lies.

People say often that education has the potential of being the great leveler in society and a huge source of positive change and progress for all. It can be so if administered properly by governments. It is also said by some people, especially by those of us in the field of education, that it is a human right and not a privilege. Sadly, to this day, many governments around the world still do their utmost to keep as many of their citizens as possible in the dark, in almost abject ignorance, in order to better control and exploit them to satisfy their own leaders' selfish goals. Sooner or later, however, history has shown that this ill-conceived plan impacts negatively on those countries' economy, possible societal improvements and general progress, which will keep them underdeveloped and poor. There is still much work to be done in the area of education worldwide for the good of all humanity.

EPILOGUE

In conclusion, António's death took place at the Paramount Hotel, in New York, on August 22nd, 1961, very far away from Ponta Delgada, São Miguel, Azores, where he had arrived from Boston the day before accompanied by Laura, a married woman who lived in Somerville, one of Boston's suburbs. He was forty-three years old and, according to the official autopsy that was mandated by law by the State of New York because he had passed away in a public place, and because of his age, and because of the fact that he was a Portuguese government civil servant, he died of laryngeal edema. What brought it about? Was it a natural death or was it perhaps the deliberate result of poisoning? I have wondered often about this last possibility, just like Elzira and the rest of her family did when it happened. But, unlike my mother, I do not believe that Laura had much to do with it. Instead, I tend to side to some extent with the male relatives and friends of the family who felt that Aníbal had been, perhaps, involved in the tragic event. They were convinced, although they lacked the necessary evidence to corroborate their firmly held belief, that he had played a role in António's demise to avenge himself. And they justified their hypothesis by claiming that humans, possessed by their emotions and incapable of sound judgement, are capable of anything and everything, including, if need be, cold-blooded murder. I, on the other hand, remain skeptical to this day about their theory, one, like I said, that was entirely based on their gut feeling for they could not prove anything.

The least that can be surmised about the tragic turn of events for António, is that his destiny had started to unravel for quite some time beforehand. In fact, one might even go so far as to suggest that it all started to disentangle with his own birth on September 20th, 1917. His fate was sealed on that day and, going forward, the universe just unfolded as it should. In other words, he became a pawn at the hands of Fate and, although he thought that he was the only one who was in full control of his own destiny, his life was in fact governed by forces beyond his sole control. He experienced, for a few days in 1961, a much written about theme in literature, *ménage à trois*, and paid the price for it perhaps by becoming the target of a personal vendetta.

According to Laura, who was constantly with António during his last two days alive, he had been displaying unusual nervousness and was most anxious to conclude as quickly as possible his business transactions. The failure to have sealed the deal concerning the fava beans satisfactorily during the first trip to New York on Thursday and Friday of the previous week definitely brought about added stress to his life and it did not help in any way shape or form his health status which had been deteriorating fast ever since Sunday evening, August 20th, the day he started complaining about a throat problem and other issues. He felt very tired and short of breath. He was experiencing some of the tell-tale signs of, for instance, sodium nitrite poisoning such as: cyanosis, hypoxia, dysrhythmia. He felt very tired and short of breath. Did these symptoms come about as the result of a poison-laced drink of some kind during that weekend? Nobody will ever know the answer to this question.

What is known for sure, though, is that António was indeed a very proud Azorean. He believed that the Azores had much to offer to the world; not only its natural and unspoiled beauty, but also many of its flavorful local products. Regarding the former, he knew intimately his native island of São Miguel and never missed an opportunity to brag about its iconic viewpoints such as Lagoa das Sete Cidades, Lagoa das Furnas, Lagoa do Fogo, Lagoa do Congro, Miradouro de Santa Iria, Ponta da Madrugada, and so many other lovely places to be found all over the island. He had also travelled throughout the Azores and knew that each one of the other eight islands was unique and beautiful in its own way. As for the latter, in his official letterhead, he mentions a few of them: chicory, eddoes, fava beans, kidney beans, green peas, onions, peanuts, pineapples, potatoes, etc. He was also convinced that there would be an international market for canned fish from São Miguel, especially tuna. António was a man who dared to dream about a better future for himself and his family and, indirectly, for his fellow Azoreans but who, sadly, was crushed by a cruel destiny much too soon.

His life was, as Calderón put it so well, a *frenesí*, a frenzy, and his *sueño* was just that, a dream, an *ilusión* an illusion, one that just did not have time to materialize. His lifespan, because of its shortness, can be described as a *sombra*, a shadow of a life. That said, in his short life, he did have the chance to experience love, fatherhood, the friendship of many friends, success as a competent, appreciated, loyal and trusted public servant and even, to a certain extent, that of a part-time businessman. When all is said and done, what does matter in the end is the quality and not the quantity of one's experiences in life.

Perhaps that as António faced death on that early morning of August 22nd, 1961, he would have agreed with his fellow countryman Eça de Queirós, the most important Portuguese novelist of the XIX century, a disciple of the great Zola who, through the words of Carlos da Maia, in the novel *Os Maias*, arrives at the cynical conclusion that: *Com efeito, não vale a pena fazer nada, correr com ânsia para coisa alguma.* (Indeed, it's not worth it to do anything, be anxious about anything.) And his best friend, Egas, completes his thought by adding: *Nem para o amor, nem para a glória, nem para o dinheiro, nem para o poder...* (Not for love, not for glory, not for money, not for power...)

As for me, I do not share Eça's main characters' philosophy of life. I, on the other hand, prefer to side with Saint-Exupéry who, through the fox in *Le Petit Prince*, reveals to the young prince a secret of considerable significance about humans lost on this vast Earth: *On ne voit bien qu'avec le cœur. L'essentiel est invisible pour les yeux.* When it comes to human behavior, in spite of one's rational training, sometimes the truth lies elsewhere and, therefore, it cannot be explained logically if at all. In order to grasp people's motives and behavior, one has to resort to one's intuition and feelings about them. People are the biggest mystery of them all and nothing that is said about their feelings, thought processes and actions can be put forward with certainty, and much less with authority. Every individual is made up of contradictions, some more obvious than others and, therefore, there can only be some ambivalence when stating anything about their persona.

Mitch Albom, in his curious novel entitled *The Five People You Meet in Heaven*, imagines the possibility of one meeting in heaven five people who, by some chance encounter here on Earth with a particular individual, changed the course of that person's life for the better although at the time the person was unaware of it.

In my case, if that opportunity were offered to me, I would like to meet again, or for the first time, the following people: António, my dear father, who was so good to me during the brief time that we shared and whose voice I have forgotten over the years. Even though his life was short, he had a full life in that he went through all sorts of experiences, both personal and professional, that enriched him as a person and, in the process, all those around him. In the final analysis, perhaps António would agree that the most important ones among them were the love and devotion of a wife and the pleasures of fatherhood. But really, who knows for certain?

Next in line, I would love to see again Elzira, my dearest mother, who sacrificed everything for me because she was protective, unselfish, generous and always kind. She continued to be faithful to the love of her life from the moment that she became a widow until her own death in 1981. She had the foresight to carefully preserve the documentation connected to António's untimely death hoping that one day I would take a closer look at it and draw some conclusions based on it. This book, without her help, would not have been possible.

I would also be grateful to encounter again my maternal grandmother Margarida who was always gentle and bighearted towards me when I needed it the most. From her weekly miserly allowance to buy the necessities of life, she used to save a few *escudos* to give me so that I could go to the movies on Sunday afternoons at the Cine Marítimo, a neighborhood cinema that existed back then in Ponta Delgada. Thanks to her, I was able, as a young boy, to escape momentarily a reality at home that was not always the most pleasant.

And, of course, I would want to meet face to face Laura, the woman at the center of this tragic story, the woman who caused so much grief and pain to my mother when I was growing up and who was directly blamed for António's fate together with her husband. For her, I would have only one simple question: was it her decision not to be buried with her husband in 2001 or someone else's? If it was hers, it's a decision that defies logic unless, of course, there was a very good reason for it to have been made. She had lots of time to think about her final resting place between 1975, the year her husband died, and 2001, when she passed away. The fact remains that she is resting for eternity with António and not with her husband.

And last but not least, I would certainly look forward to a rendezvous with the old barber. If, indeed, he carried out his revenge plan as presumed in this book, it would have been executed during the weekend of August 19th, 1961. He would have done it out of rage for the audacity of a woman, his wife, who had deceived him so brazenly with another man. He had brought her to America. He had saved her from a life of mediocrity in São Miguel, a woman, so he thought, who should have been eternally grateful to him for his generosity, who should have been faithful to him for the rest of his life. I would love to ascertain, once and for all, if the hypothesis developed in this narrative is correct or if it is, instead, flawed. I would be keen to know if the members and friends of the Faria family who were most familiar with the events surrounding António's death, especially Virgínio and his two sons, and who blamed him for it, underestimated his capacity to love a woman to such an extent that he was willing, just to have her around, to turn a blind eye on her infidelity and do nothing about it. If that were to be the case, it would have meant that when he had permitted his wife to travel to New York in the company of a man much younger than himself, it was because he had complete confidence in her moral integrity which, of course, would have made it impossible for her to betray him under any circumstances, even when left alone in a hotel room with a man whom she still loved and for whom she had always felt physically attracted to ever since she was a teenager. In short, finding out that his involvement in António's demise was a mere figment of my relatives' twisted imagination and that, instead, his death had been brought about by some catastrophic allergy reaction aggravated by many years of heavy smoking and a heart so weak that it just could not take stress anymore, would be a most welcome piece of news. If, however, their theory turned out to be sound, I would inquire if he lived in peace with himself until his death.

But, alas, the dead carry with them to the other world most of their secrets and our chances of meeting them in heaven are nothing short of remote. Consequently, we, the living, are left with the impossible task, a puzzle really, of putting together individual pieces that do not quite fit together perfectly. The process of arranging and rearranging them until the whole image looks plausible consumes our time, exhausts our energy, tests our patience, demands insight into human behavior and, ultimately, when everything is said and done, the puzzle can only be resolved in our minds with a great deal of imagination because the individual pieces will never fit flawlessly. Nothing that is ever said about human beings can be assumed to be foolproof. So, I am afraid that the uncertainty concerning António's real cause of death will remain forever a mystery.

That being said, it's spellbinding the impact that two total strangers, Laura and Aníbal, two individuals whom I do not recall ever meeting personally, but whom I seem to know well enough through a variety of secondary sources, had on my life trajectory. My personality was forever shaped by the events surrounding my father's unexpected and sudden death in the US in 1961 and by the people who played major roles in the unfolding of the tragedy.

EPILOGUE

But, despite the tragedy that occurred early on in my life and that literally ruined Elzira's in her prime, both of us slowly came to the realization that we were loved and cherished, to the best of his ability, by this proud Azorean named António Augusto Machado whose life was a true *frenesí* and the briefest of *sueños*.

The decision, in my late sixties, to write about the life and death of a man who played such a pivotal and indelible role in my childhood, albeit ever so briefly, was not taken lightly. Although António only participated directly on my own earthly journey until I turned nine, his kindness, generosity, friendship and, most importantly, his unconditional love for me, helped create the kind of man that I eventually became in spite of all the inevitable *contretemps* that ensued after his death. In trying to do justice to his memory, as Pagnol put it so well in the foreword of *La Gloire de mon père*, the challenge was to figure out what position to assume as the memorialist within the narrative. Not an easy task for any individual who attempts to embark on a project of the sort, especially one who is a novice in the art of story-telling for it is, literally, a minefield that if stepped on inadvertently, can blow the project to pieces at any given moment. Therefore, one has to proceed gently, cautiously, and at one's own risk.

I am Roberto Augusto Machado, the narrator of this story, one that is only partly true since it's also a work of fiction at times. It's a story that has been an integral part of my reality ever since August 22nd, 1961, when I was an ordinary, happy-go-lucky and carefree little boy. That fateful day, life's hidden threads unraveled of their own accord.

May António, Elzira, Laura, Aníbal and all the other people who played a major part in this narrative, directly or indirectly, rest in peace wherever they may be.

Amen.

ACKNOWLEDGMENTS

The writing of *The Life and Death of a Proud Azorean: A Biography* would not have been possible without the presence in my life of some key people. Therefore, thanks are in order to the following individuals: first and foremost, to my dear mother for keeping for decades the documentation, photographs, the 8 mm film taken at António's funeral, and some of the belongings that my father valued the most. This treasure trove was most valuable to me as I drafted this manuscript. All along, deep down in her heart, my mother knew that if I lived long enough, I would one day use the material that she kept so very carefully in some fashion, perhaps even write a book based on its contents. Needless to say, she guessed it right. If she were alive, I wonder what she would have said about the way in which I fashioned this particular storyline.

Next, I have to credit my father for loving me as much as he did for the first nine years of my life. What he did in that short period of time was enough to sustain me for the rest of my own life journey. One might say that he planted the seeds of confidence in me, seeds that with time produced many fruits, both professional and personal. Above everything else, António valued education, especially higher education, something that, sadly, had not been available to him and that had limited his professional advancement as a civil servant. I think that he would have been proud of my accomplishments in the realm of education. Of course, he was absolutely right in thinking that a good degree opens all sorts of professional opportunities that either directly or indirectly impact on a person's quality of life. By following his advice, I have enjoyed a very fulfilling existence.

ACKNOWLEDGMENTS

Also, I do have to put in a word of thanks to all my other family members who have passed away and who were, just like all human beings, people with a combination of personality flaws, but also capable of acts of kindness and love. Among them stands out my maternal grandmother Margarida and one of her sons, my uncle João; she was kindness personified and he was fun to be with at all times. Both were invaluable to a boy who lost his father unexpectedly.

Finally, I would like to thank my wife and daughter for not only putting up with me and my idiosyncrasies, but also for their support all along in my many and varied endeavors; they have demonstrated the patience of saints for which I am eternally grateful. *Obrigado*.

PHOTOGRAPH CREDITS

Photography Insert

All photographs courtesy of the Machado Family Archives

APPENDIX

Copia   Telegrama Recebido no dia 22 de Agosto de 1961

Governador Civil de Ponta Delgada

António Augusto Machado faleceu hoje hotel Nova Iorque Stop. Indispensável conhecer decisão família acerca lugar funeral ou transporte corpo Ponta Delgada Favor telegrafar instruções prima do falecido Laura Jesse

                Consul Geral

Copy of the official telegram from the Portuguese Consulate in New York to the Governor of the Autonomous District of Ponta Delgada announcing António's death, August 22nd, 1961.

S. R.

Junta Geral do Distrito Autónomo
de
Ponta Delgada
(Secretaria)

Exma. Senhora
D. Maria Elzira Faria Machado
Rua da Boa Nova, 82
Ponta Delgada

Sua referência: Sua comunicação de: Nossa referência: Ponta Delgada, (data)
                                        1499   24-8-1961

Assunto:

Cumpre-me o dever de comunicar a V.Exª. que a Comissão Executiva deste Corpo Administrativo, na sua reunião da presente data, deliberou registar na respectiva acta um voto de muito pesar pelo inesperado falecimento de seu marido, Sr. António Augusto Machado, que, sendo Informador dos Serviços de Coordenação Económica, de há anos a esta parte, vinha exercendo, com o maior aprumo e vincado zelo, as funções de encarregado da Agência de Compras desta Junta Geral.

Apresento a V.Exª. os meus cumprimentos.

A bem da Nação

O PROCURADOR SERVINDO DE PRESIDENTE

(João Hickling Anglin)

LF/MC

A letter of condolences from the president of Junta Geral do Distrito Autónomo de Ponta Delgada, Mr. João Hickling Anglin, addressed to Elzira and dated shortly after his passing.

Liceu Central de Antero de Quental

Curso geral — 1.ª Secção

Ano de 19 29 - 19 30

Classe I, turma 2.ª, n.º 3

Disciplinas	Notas de aproveitamento		Faltas	Procedimento	Rubricas
	Em algarismos	Por extenso			
Primeiro período					
Português	11	onze	1	Bom	
Francês	12	doze	1		
Geografia	12	doze	—		
Sciências	12	doze	—		
Matemática	14	catorze	1		
Desenho	10	dez	3		
Trabalhos manuais					
Canto coral	B	Bom	—		
Gimnástica	S	Suficiente	—		
Segundo período					
Português	12	doze	2	Bom	
Francês	16	dezasseis	2		
Geografia	15	quinze	1		
Sciências	16	dezasseis	2		
Matemática	17	dezassete	3		
Desenho	12	doze	2		
Trabalhos manuais					
Canto coral	B	Bom	1		
Gimnástica	S	Suficiente	—		

Page 1 of 2 from António's Caderno Escolar – Instrução Secundária, 1929-1935; an official record book of his marks, attendance and general behavior. He was a bright student.

Disciplinas	Notas de aproveitamento		Faltas	Procedimento	Rubricas
	Em algarismos	Por extenso			
Terceiro período					
Português	14	catorze	—		
Francês	16	dezasseis	—		
Geografia	13	treze	—		
Sciências	14	catorze	—	Bom	
Matemática	17	dezassete	1		
Desenho	12	doze	1		
Trabalhos manuais					
Canto coral	B	Bom	—		
Gimnástica	S	Suficiente	—		

Ficaram registadas estas notas, em virtude das quais o aluno foi admitido à classe imediata com a classificação final de catorze valores.

Em 30 de Janeiro de 1930

O Chefe da Secretaria,

Registo de transferência e outras observações

Thu a receber:
Dinheiro meu:
    201.949.40 do negócio
    14.500.00 do Alcume
    entre ao concerto de casa.

Se não houver acordo vende a casa aonde Emiliano mora.

Lucro Provável: 87.405.20.

Deste dinheiro darás ao Sr. Castelo 48.457$00 para pagamento do resto das despesas do f.r. Restarão por tanto 38.948.20.

Deste dinheiro que resta darás em gratificações ao Eduardo Valério 5.000$00 (cinco mil escudos) e 10.000$00 (dez mil escudos) ao Sr. Castelo.

P.D. 14/8/961

Page 1 of 2 of António's brief business and personal notes left for Elzira before his second trip to the US, August 14th, 1961; in it, he specifies that his wife should do her utmost to see to it that Roberto goes on to higher education; it was a wish that she faithfully carried out.

Dês questão no Tribunal de tutes, pa se poder a diferenças que a firma Morais & Pallares diz que restituiu ao Dinis Motta Soares, ele já recebeu essa diferença. Caso eu ganhe a questão o Dinis deve-me 35.300$00 (trinta e cinco mil, trezentos escudos), conforme os vales juntos.

Tens a receber mais o seguro de 500.000$00 da Comp. Européa e 75.000$00 ao Cofre de Previdenc. do Quadro Geral.

Espero que faças todo o desejo possivel para que o Roberto tire um curso superior.

[signature]

Page 2 of 2 of António's brief business and personal notes left for Elzira before his second trip to the US, August 14th, 1961; in it, he specifies that his wife should do her utmost to see to it that Roberto goes on to higher education; it was a wish that she faithfully carried out.

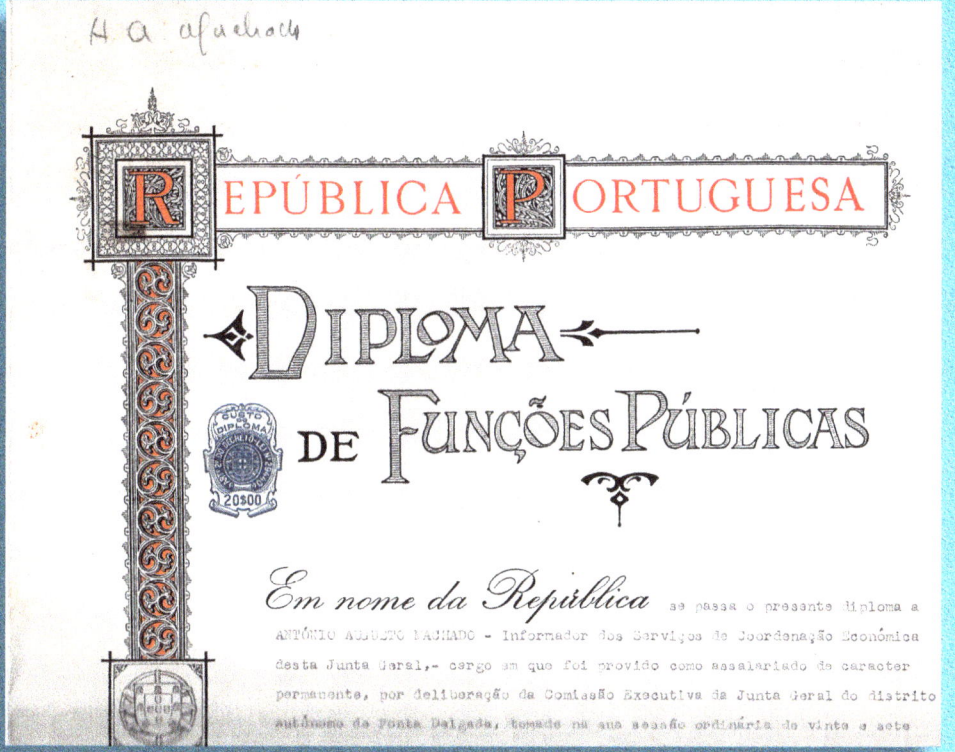

António's Diploma de Funções Públicas, February 11th, 1943; an official document from the Portuguese Republic stating that António had become a permanent member of the public service.

**COMISSÃO DISTRITAL
REGULADORA
DO
ABASTECIMENTO
DE
SUBSISTÊNCIAS**

Nº 353
Liv.º 1944

SERVIÇO DA REPÚBLICA

Ponta Delgada, 30 de Dezembro de 19 44

Ao Ex.mo Sr. António Augusto Machado

Ponta Delgada

    A Comissão da minha Presidência encarrega-me de comunicar a V.Exª. que , em sua reunião de 29 de corrente , louvou V.Exª. pelos serviços prestados como Encarregado da Secretaria desta Comissão .
    Apresento a V.Exª. os meus cumprimentos .

A BEM DA NAÇÃO

O PRESIDENTE DA COMISSÃO ,

(Victor Machado de Faria e Maia)

An official letter from Mr. Víctor Machado de Faria e Maia, President of the Committee in charge of Supplies for the Distrito Autónomo de Ponta Delgada, praising António for his services, December 30th, 1944; António was the happy recipient of many such letters from Mr. Machado de Faria e Maia.

<u>ATESTADO</u>

A Comissão Executiva da Junta Geral do distrito autónomo de Ponta Delgada atesta, em sua reunião de vinte e sete de Dezembro de mil novecentos e quarenta e oito, que o Senhor António Augusto Machado, Informador dos Serviços de Coordenação Económica desta Junta Geral, nos períodos de vinte e oito de Abril de mil novecentos e quarenta e um a dez de Fevereiro de mil novecentos e quarenta e três (no qual prestou serviços como assalariado de carácter eventual) e de onze daquele mesmo mês e ano a dezassete de Julho de mil novecentos e quarenta e quatro (como fazendo parte do quadro do pessoal assalariado permanente dos Serviços dêste Corpo Administrativo) e daquela mesma data até ao presente, na situação de destacado, por ter sido requisitado, para prestar serviço no Govêrno Civil dêste distrito, tem demonstrado sempre ser um empregado exemplarmente disciplinado, cumprindo e observando, rigorosamente, todas as instruções dos seus superiores e executando todos os serviços que lhe têm sido destinado com muito zêlo, competência e aptidão, qualidades que o recomendam para qualquer outro serviço de maior responsabilidade.---

Sala das Sessões da Comissão Executiva da Junta Geral do distrito autónomo de Ponta Delgada, 27 de Dezembro de 1948

A COMISSÃO EXECUTIVA

Page 2 of 2 A letter from Junta Geral dated December 27, 1948, detailing António's job assignments until then as well as praising him for his competence, dedication, loyalty, etc.

S. R.

GOVERNO CIVIL DO DISTRITO AUTÓNOMO
DE
PONTA DELGADA

ORDEM DE SERVIÇO Nº 9

    Louvo o funcionário da Junta Geral em serviço neste Governo Civil, ANTÓNIO AUGUSTO MACHADO, que, durante muitos anos, tem desempenhado, com a maior honestidade e proficiência, as funções de encarregado do abastecimento de subsistências, no exercício das quais revelou sempre a maior dedicação e zelo, conduzindo-se por forma a merecer, mesmo em delicadas e difíceis situações, a consideração e a estima dos seus superiores hierárquicos, bem como daqueles com quem teve de estar em contacto.

    Governo Civil do distrito autónomo de Ponta Delgada, 23 de Novembro de 1954.

O Governador do distrito

(Aniceto António dos Santos)

An official letter from the Governor of the Autonomous District of Ponta Delgada, Mr. Aniceto dos Santos, commending António for his loyalty, dedication, professionalism and "savoir-faire", November 23rd, 1954; the governor, who was from mainland Portugal, developed a strong friendship with António and counted on him for advice on matters regarding the personality and character of his subordinates during his tenure in Ponta Delgada.

Modêlo n.º 459 do Catálogo—Diversos
(Da Imprensa Nacional de Lisboa)

CADASTRO GERAL DOS FUNCIONÁRIOS DO ESTADO

Número de ordem _____

Nome ___ António Augusto Machado ___
Filho de ___ Manuel Augusto Cristiano Machado ___ e de ___ Maria Eulália do Carmo Machado ___
Data do nascimento 20/ 9 / 917 Categoria ___ Informador dos Serviços de Coordenação Económica da Junta Geral ___
Ministério _____ Direcção _____
_____ Serviço Serviços de Coordenação Económica
Vencimento mensal _____ $ Data da primeira nomeação 11/ 2 / 43
Habilitações literárias 4º. anos dos Liceus _____

Outros cargos exercidos de 1º de Julho de 1944 destacado no Govêrno Civil como Encarregado da Secretaria da Comissão Distrital Reguladora do Abastecimento de Subsistências; de 12 de Junho de 1948 como Encarregado da Secção de Abastecimentos do mesmo Govêrno Civil, lugar que acumula ainda com o de Encarregado da Agência de Compras da Junta Geral desde 25 de Janeiro de 1951 por deliberação da Exma. Comissão Executiva.

Promovido a _____ em ___/___/___ vencimento _____ $ _____
Promovido a _____ em ___/___/___ vencimento _____ $ _____
Promovido a _____ em ___/___/___ vencimento _____ $ _____
Promovido a _____ em ___/___/___ vencimento _____ $ _____
Promovido a _____ em ___/___/___ vencimento _____ $ _____

Modêlo n.º 61 — T. C.

Page 1 of 2 António's Cadastro Geral dos Funcionários Públicos; an official record of António's government assignments from 1944-1961.

Outros cargos exercidos de 15 de Julho de 1944 destacado no Governo Civil como Encarregado da Secretaria da Comissão Distrital Reguladora do Abastecimento de Subsistências; de 12 de Junho de 1948 como Encarregado da Secção de Abastecimentos do mesmo Governo Civil, lugar que acumula ainda com o de encarregado da Agência de Compras da Junta Geral desde 25 de Janeiro de 1951 por deliberação da Exma. Comissão Executiva.

Promovido a _____ em __/__/__ vencimento _____$
Promovido a _____ em __/__/__ vencimento _____$
Promovido a _____ em __/__/__ vencimento _____$
Promovido a _____ em __/__/__ vencimento _____$
Promovido a _____ em __/__/__ vencimento _____$

Transferido para _____ em __/__/__
Transferido para _____ em __/__/__
Transferido para _____ em __/__/__
Transferido para _____ em __/__/__
Transferido para _____ em __/__/__

Demitido em __/__/__
Readmitido em __/__/__
Aposentado em __/__/__
Falecido em __/__/__

Observações: De 17 de Agosto de 1939 a 27 de Abril de 1941, prestou serviço no Posto de Sanidade Vegetal com zêlo, assiduidade e competência (atestado do Exmo. Director da Estação Agrária em 29/Nov/48) -28 de Abril de 1941 a 10 de Fevereiro de 1943 (como assalariado de carácter eventual) e de 11 de Fevereiro de 1943 a 17 de Julho de 1944 (como assalariado de carácter permanente) e daquela mesma data até 27 de Dezembro de 1948, como destacado no Governo Civil demonstrou muito zêlo, competência e aptidão (atestado da Exma. Comissão Executiva de 27 de Dezembro de 1948)-30 de Dezº.44, louvado pela Exma. C.D.P.A. Subsistências (ofício nº. 353 Lº.1944)-2 Fevereiro.45, idem, idem (ofício nº.449-Lº.1945-10 Outº.946, nomeado por Sua EXª.o Governador para receber o material Sanitário do Hospital Militar para a Assistência (ofº.598-C)

segue verso

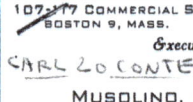

Nov. 18, 1960

A. Augusto Machado
Ponta Delgada
S. Miguel Acores

Gentlemen:

We thank you for your letter of Nov. 2nd, and we were indeed sorry that you could not spend more time with us, when you were in Boston. However, we shall look forward to your next visit.

We hope that we can do substanial business with you when the new fave are ready.

CASEIN: This item is out of our line, and we are sorry that we can do anything for you with it.

BEANS: Besides fave, we sell a substanial quantity of Italian white kidney beans, and also chick peas both from Italy and Portugal. These probably are the only type beans that we can develope any business for you.

Kindest regards from all.

Yours very truly,

Musolino Lo Conte Co.

A. J. Musolino

AJM:dm

A Musolino Co. letter to António, November 18th, 1960; António did the bulk of his export business with this import/export company with branches in Boston and New York.

L. N. WHITE & COMPANY, INC. • *Import and Export*

CABLE ADDRESS
"ELENWHITE" N.Y.

24 STONE STREET
NEW YORK 4, N. Y.
•
PHONE BOWLING GREEN 9-7363

August 3, 1961

A. Augusto Machado
Rua Da Boa Noya 82
Ponta Delgada, S. Miguel, Azores

Dear Mr. Machado:

We wish to acknowledge receipt of your cable regarding our interest in purchasing Azores Fava Beans this year.

We are interested in Fava Beans, but are reluctant to purchase any this year as we understand that there has been purchases made from the Azores at various prices. In addition, there are a number of brokers here who are offering to the small buyers Azores Fava Beans from their principals in Portugal as well as the Azores.

When you were in New York last, we gave you a complete picture as to the market conditions here and showed you that there is no room for at least a half dozen people offering Fava Beans creating a competition which is not there. Actually the requirements in the United States is approximately 3500 to 4000 bags. In view of this small quantity and this being a specialty bean, we would be interested if we could handle the United States and Canada on an exclusive basis.

As mentioned above, we know that there has been purchases made from the Azores, so that exclusivity for this year is out. We would, however, like to have a sample of the larger size favas which you are offering as well as your best price CIF New York.

At this writing, we are taking the opportunity to remind you during our conversation here in New York that we are interested in Casein. We believe that if the quality and prices are right, we may be able to handle the entire production from your Country.

Awaiting your reply with interest, we are,

Very truly yours,

L.N. WHITE & COMPANY, INC.

SM/ar
VIA AIRMAIL

A letter sent by the L. N. White Co. to António on August 3rd, 1961; next to the Musolino Co., this company showed interest in doing business with António.

Two postcards sent from the Abbey Hotel in New York, August 18th, 1961; António and Laura stayed in this hotel during their first trip to the Big Apple; the hotel, built in 1927, was demolished in 1982.

António Augusto Machado

Endereço Address-Rua da Boa Nova, 82 — Telefone Telephone 22414
Telegramas Cable Address-Anauma-Pontadelgada — Caixa Postal P. O. Box 42

Exportador Exporter

Amendoim	Peanut
Batata	Potato
Cebola	Onion
Chicória	Chicory
Ervilha	Pea
Fava	Fava-Bean
Feijão	Kidney-Bean
Inhames	Desheens

Visitar da Emília e Família

Somerville, Mass. 20/8/961

Querida Elzira

Deus permita que te encontres bem, assim como o Roberto. Felizmente, eu estou bem, mas cansado, digo, até mesmo bastante cansado por causa das favas. O navio ainda não as descarregou todas e, portanto, ainda não sei se as sacas que estavam em falta, embarcaram ou não.

Desde quarta-feira que, muito cedo, quinta-feira até ontem, estive em New York. Tem-me acompanhado a Laura e o João Girando. Este é um trapalhão muito grande a falar o inglês, mas a Laura que o fala muitíssimo bem, é que nos tem salvo de situações que nos poderiam prejudicar. Tem sido incansável. O Mário também estava para ir connosco a New York mas, como esteve doente aqueles 4 meses, disse-me que lhe era totalmente impossível deslocar-se nesta altura, para não ter que fechar mais uma vez a Barbearia.

Amanhã, voltamos os 3 novamente a New York e espero voltar ainda mesmo amanhã, se as coisas correrem bem.

Apesar do João Girando se encontrar com a melhor disposição em me ajudar, ele está-me a complicar a vida

Todas as ofertas são sujeitas a confirmação = All offers are always subject to confirmation

Page 1 of 2: António's last letter to Elzira; it was written on Sunday, August 20th, 1961, two days before his passing using his stationery; in it, among many other subjects, António claims that he is extremely tired and lies repeatedly about who is traveling with him to New York; this letter is analyzed in great detail in the book.

porque sempre quero os 500 sacos e, estou mesmo a ver que vai ser pesado. Enfim Deus há de permitir que as coisas hão de correr pelo melhor.

Por aqui a atmosfera é de guerra. Por onde quer que nos encontramos, vêm-se soldados e marinheiros. Não sei como irá acabar esta história de Berlim.

Elzira deves ter recebido ontem ou anteontem à tarde um telegrama. Terás tu compreendido o que ele te dizia. Trata-se o seguinte:

Dizer ao Valério que mandasse o Castelo e o Guilherme arcarem a fazer de embalar, que as terão e se este não der para os 250 ou 300 sacos que quero que compres pelo melhor preço.

Pede ao Valério que te ponha em contacto com o Dinis Justo e lhe pergunte se já receber a licença de distro. Caso os tenha recebido estas faras (250 ou 300) sacos devem ser despachadas com a licença dele e o Castelo que trate do despacho.

Ele deve dizer ao Dinis que ainda são um mundo as suas foras porque o White não está em New York e só chega amanhã. Infelizmente para ele o Marsolais de Conte não quer mais e os outros que se mostraram interessados compraram ao no Conte.

O Valério que me avance as amostras de conservas de peixe, saiba o preço que eles fazem posto aqui em New York e não se esqueça de perguntar qual a comissão que os fabricantes nos dão. Este pedido é urgente.

Eles aqui estão muito interessados nisto.

Agora, minha querida, diz-me como tens passado? O Yoyo tem-se estado bem? Ainda não pude falar com a mãe dele mas já falei com o Humberto. E o teu tio, já escrito? Tens tido animado? Toste os miúdos? Tens te dado ele? Escrev-em para que tipo de escrever, muitos e muitos beijos para muitos e cem
_____

Page 2 of 2: António's last letter to Elzira; it was written on Sunday, August 20th, 1961, two days before his passing using his stationery; in it, among many other subjects, António claims that he is extremely tired and lies repeatedly about who is traveling with him to New York; this letter is analyzed in great detail in the book.

MINISTÉRIO DA JUSTIÇA N.º _____

CONSERVATÓRIA DOS REGISTOS CENTRAIS

BOLETIM DE ÓBITO

No dia 22 de Agosto de 1961 pelas _____ horas, em Nova Iorque, Distrito de Manhattan _____ faleceu António A. Machado _____ filho de Manuel A. Machado _____ e de Maria Pacheco _____ como consta da transcrição de óbito n.º 136, lavrada nesta Conservatória aos 10 de Março de 1952.

Lx. 10 de Março de 1952.

O Ajudante

[assinatura] Idalina da Loureira Fernandes

Modelo n.º 12 da Cons. dos Reg. Centrais

Death Certificate as issued by Ministério da Justiça, Conservatória dos Registos Centrais, issued on March 10th, 1962.

KIRKLAND 7-0400　　　　　　　　　　　　　　　　　　　　　TROWBRIDGE 6-0400
157 PROSPECT ST.　　　　　　　　　　　　　　　　　　　　　1643 CAMBRIDGE ST.

JOSEPH A. COSTA SONS

P. O. BOX ONE
CAMBRIDGE 39, MASSACHUSETTS

Mrs. Laura Jesse
243 Powder House Boulevard,
Somerville, Massachusetts

FUNERAL EXPENSES OF:

" ANTONIO AUGUSTO MACHADO "
Deceased August 22, 1961　　　Interment August 30, 1961

Casket	$435.00
Grave Liner for Casket	85.00
Removal of Remains, South Station, Boston, Mass. to Cambridge, Massachusetts	20.00
Staff Services and Supervision of Funeral	50.00
	$590.00
Returning Shipping Case, Boston to New York City	10.32
Funeral Notices Boston Globe Newspaper	19.20
Telephone and Telegram Charges to New York City	9.86
St. Anthony's Church Mass Offering	35.00
Offering to Priest at Grave	5.00
Opening Grave, Cambridge Cemetery, Cambridge, Mass.	45.00
Hearse to Cambridge Cemetery	30.00
Limousine to Cambridge Cemetery	20.00
	174.38

NEW YORK FUNERAL SERVICE INC. CHARGES

Procuring death certificate-burial-transit permit licensed Funeral Director, service car to transfer remains City Mortuary to chapel 148 East 74th St., Embalming-complete autopsy-place remains in transfer case, service car and assistant to Railroad	95.00
Underwear and socks	2.75
Railroad fare to South Station, Boston, Mass.	27.98
Man to Consul General of Portugal, 630 Fifth Ave., New York City for release paper from Public Administrator, New York County	5.00
Help at Railroad Depot and Mortuary	3.00
New York to Massachusetts phone calls	2.25
	135.98

Total Expenses --------- $900.36

Oct. 23, 1961
Received from Mrs. Laura Jesse $460.00
Unpaid Balance $440.36
George J. Costa

Received Payment
Joseph A. Costa Sons
By _____

António's funeral bill, August 30th, 1961; the arrangements were carried out by the Joseph A. Costa Sons Memorial Funeral Home located in Cambridge, Massachusetts.

Hotel Paramount
FORTY-SIXTH STREET (WEST OF BROADWAY)
NEW YORK 36. N. Y.

MACHADO—In New York city, Aug. 22, Antonio A. of Ponta Delgada, Azores, Portugal. Beloved husband of Elzira (Faria) and cousin of Mr. and Mrs. Eneval Jesse, Mrs. Fernanda Mendonca, Adelaide Asadoorian. Funeral from the Joseph A. Costa Sons Memorial Funeral Home, 1643 Cambridge st., Cambridge, cor. Trowbridge st., Wednesday, Aug. 30, at 8 a.m. Solemn High Mass at St. Anthony's Church, Portland st., Cambridge, at 9 a.m. Relatives and friends invited to attend. Calling hours 2 to 4 and 7 to 10 p.m.

Necrologia
FALECIMENTOS

António Augusto Machado

Faleceu num hotel em Nova Iorque, o sr. António Augusto Machado, que ali se encontrava há uma semana e era informador dos Serviços de Coordenação Económica da Junta Geral, desempenhando ùltimamente as funções de agente de compras daquele corpo administrativo,

Contando apenas 43 anos de idade o extinto, pelas suas qualidades de trabalho e de afabilidade, desfrutava, entre o funcionalismo da Junta Geral e no nosso meio, de consideração e de estima, sendo por isso muito sentida a sua morte inesperada.

Era casado com a sr.a D. Maria Elzira de Faria Machado; pai do menino Roberto Augusto de Faria Cristiano Machado filho da sr.a D. Maria Eulália do Carmo Machado, genro do sr. Virgínio Faria, proprietário de automóveis de praça, irmão dos srs. José Cristiano Machado, funcionário da Companhia Portuguesa Rádio Marconi, e do sr. Cristiano Augusto Machado, funcionário da Intendência de Pecuária, e cunhado do sr. Henrique Carvalho Valério, chefe da Secretaria da Câmara Municipal de Vila do Porto.

A toda a família, as nossas condolências.

António's obituaries as they appeared in the Boston Globe and the Açoreano Oriental.

S.  R.

GOVERNO CIVIL DO DISTRITO AUTÓNOMO DE PONTA DELGADA

Exma. Senhora
D. Alzira Faria Machado
P O N T A D E L G A D A

Sua referência:	Sua comunicação de:	Nossa referência:	Ponta Delgada (data)
		905-C-26	25-9-961

ASSUNTO:

Encarrega-me Sua Exª. o Governador de transmitir a V. Exª. o ofício nº. 382, Proc.7, de 6 do corrente, do Consulado-Geral de Portugal em New York, que a seguir se transcreve:

" Em aditamento ao meu telegrama de 23 de Agosto findo e em resposta ao de V. Exª. Nº. 160 da mesma data, cumpre-me informar que o Administrador do Condado de New York tomou posse dos objectos de uso pessoal do Senhor António Augusto Machado, falecido nesta cidade no Hotel Paramount no passado dia 22.
Mais informo V. Exª. de que no dia 25 finalmente consegui, depois de aturadas diligências e com o valioso auxílio do advogado deste Consulado Geral, Senhor Dr. Jerome Teich, obter que a referida autoridade local entregasse, ao agente funerário escolhido pela Senhora Laura Jesse, à ordem deste Consulado Geral, o cadaver do finado que ainda se encontrava depositado na morgue desta cidade. Ao mesmo tempo, foram entregues a um funcionário desta Chancelaria pela Repartição do Administrador Público os seguintes objectos de uso pessoal recolhidos pela polícia no quarto que o falecido ocupava no hotel.
a) Uma carteira de couro com o escudo nacional contendo o passaporte nº. 1967/60 emitido por esse Governo Civil e o Bilhete de Identidade nº. 377428-B, emitido pelo Arquivo de Identificação de Lisboa em 1 de Março de 1954.
b) Uma carteira de couro contendo duas chaves pequeninas, 2 cartas e 2 fotografias.
c) Um envelope contendo $64.00 (sessenta e quatro) dólares canadianos.
d) Dois aneis de metal de cor de ouro.
e) Um relógio de pulso marca Omega, modelo "Automatic Seamaster" com pulseira e caixa em metal de cor de our

Page 1 of 2 Letter from the Governo Civil do Distrito Autónomo de Ponta Delgada, dated September 25th, 1961, based on the one sent from the Consulado-Geral de Portugal in New York detailing António's possessions as found by the New York police officers at the time of his death at the Paramount Hotel.

S. R.

GOVERNO CIVIL DO DISTRITO AUTÓNOMO DE PONTA DELGADA

-2-

f) Uma caneta de tinta permanente marca Parker com côrpo cinzento e tampa de metal dourado.
g) Uma máquina fotográfica " Agfa " modelo Solinette II com lentes G 66 034.

Quanto ao dinheiro em dólares americanos que o falecido tinha consigo - e que a Senhora Laura Jesse declarou ser superior a quatrocentos dólares - o Administrador Público só os entregará, por cheque pagável à ordem deste Consulado Geral, quando lhe for apresentada, prova documental de que o falecido foi enterrado e as despesas incorridas com o funeral pagas ao respectivo agente funerário.

A pasta com documentos comerciais e uma maleta com a pouca roupa que o falecido trouxera de Masschusetts para New York foram entregues directamente pela Polícia à Senhora Laura Jesse.

Cumpre-me ainda informar que no dia 28 a Senhora Laura Jesse, pelo telefone, informou este Consulado Geral de que receberá procuração da viuva outorgando-lhe poderes para tratar do funeral e recolher os bens do falecido.

Nestes termos foi-lhe indicado de que deveria enviar a esta Chancelaria cópia da procuração para lhe serem entregues os objectos de uso pessoal e dinheiro arrecadados nesta Chancelaria.

Quanto aos negócios que o Senhor António Augusto Machado estava a tratar nesta cidade, lamento em nada poder ser útil à viuva visto este Consulado Geral não ter qualquer conhecimento deles e nem mesmo ter pessoal ou facilidades que se pudessem ocupar de tal assunto.

Apresento a V. Exª. os meus cumprimentos.

A bem da Nação

Pelo Exmo. Secretário do Governo Civil
O 3º. Oficial

(Arnaldo Saúl Teixeira)

Agosto 30-61

Querida Elzira

Que Deus me dê forças para começar esta carta, não o fiz mais cedo por ser impossível de suportar a dor de te estar a contar da morte de Antonio quando ainda se encontra entre nós, e tão longe deste mundo.

Farei por ser breve mas como me pedem pormenores, não tenho outro remedio do que contar-te como tudo aconteceu. Foi assim:

Antonio chegou na terça-feira á uma e cinco da tarde, escusado será dizer-te que o esperavamos radiantes de alegria. Val julgava que Roberto tambem viesse ficou um pouco desapontado, mas Antonio disse-lhe que tinha que ficar contigo para não ficares sozinha. depois da explicação Val ficou como nada fosse, mas muito satisfeito por ver Antonio. Falamos trocando impressões da ilha falamos na fazenda e por ele soube que não te encontravas ainda boa. A noite da terça-feira (ou seja da chegada) minha irmã Henaid veio cá e passamos uma noite mais ou menos agradavel na quarta-feira como era o dia fora de Anibal aproveitamos para lhe fazer a surpreza de ir ver a prima Tenina da de Albergaria-A-Velha, que aqui se encontra de visita. Demoramos pouco tempo, porque Antonio tinha que ir a Boston falar com a Co. que fazia negocio. Jantamos fora em Boston, e depois chegamos a casa, fomos visitar minha mãi e Henaid e lá estivemos um pouco Voltamos a casa e estivemos um pouco a ver o televisão Como Antonio tinha que ir a N. York por causa dos negocio, pediu ao Anibal para ir a N. York com ele. Anibal fazia isto de boa vontade, mas como teve a

Page 1 of 2: Two pages from Laura's second letter to Elzira in which she describes in great detail Antonio's passing at the Paramount Hotel in New York on August 22nd, and his funeral in Boston on August 30th, 1961, among many other tidbits of relevant information about his last few days.

e não o queria deixar no corredor, nem sequer abrir a porta.

Sentou-se na minha cama, e não podia respirar bem; eu fazia por o confortar o melhor possível, quando êle me pega na mão e diz Laura... queria-me dizer qualquer coisa mas já não podia. Como vi que êle ia cair e talvez magoar-se na cabeça da cama, estendi depressa os braços para o amparar, e assim suspirou e foi o fim de Antonio, que será recordado por muito tempo. Ainda julgava que estava passado num ataque de qualquer espécie, mas reparando que o coração não batia, comecei num grito medonho, a pedir socorro segundos passados, vi tanta policia, tanto homem de roda de mim que não sei explicar. E então que aquêles policias de New York são tão grandes e fortes eu parecia um gafanhoto ao pé deles. Mas Deus deu-me coragem não fiquei com medo dêles. deixaram a porta encostada e ficaram no corredor, até o médico vir, ninguém podia toca-lo. deixei-o cair na cama devagar porque não podia já com o pêso. e andei de roda do quarto sem saber o que fazer. lembrei-me dos papeis que êle tinha no seu quarto, lembrei-me das coisas que lhe pertencia, mas descancei, porque como os policias estavam no corredor não podiam roubar porque eu era testemunha dele. O medico chegou presumincion que êle estava morto, e ainda pensei ser sonho.

Mas quando me disse tem paciencia, que o Sr. Machado não sente nada, mas tu és, quem vai sentir.

Page 2 of 2: Two pages from Laura's second letter to Elzira in which she describes in great detail Antonio's passing at the Paramount Hotel in New York on August 22nd, and his funeral in Boston on August 30th, 1961, among many other tidbits of relevant information about his last few days.

ANTÓNIO AUGUSTO MACHADO
Encarregado da Secção de Abastecimentos do Governo Civil
e da Agência de Compras da Junta Geral

Rua da Boa Nova, 82   Ponta Delgada

António's business card

ABOUT THE AUTHOR

Roberto A. Machado was born in Ponta Delgada, São Miguel, Azores, in 1952. He emigrated to Canada in 1969 to avoid being drafted into the Portuguese army which was involved in an unjust war of attrition against the natives of its former colonies of Angola, Mozambique and Guiné-Bissau. He settled down in Toronto where he attended Bloor Collegiate Institute and, afterwards, the University of Toronto. He is the proud recipient of four university degrees including a Ph.D. in Québec literature. He began his teaching career in 1978 at Grand River Collegiate Institute, in Kitchener, Ontario, where he taught French and Spanish. Beginning in 1980, he taught French, Portuguese and Spanish at Harbord Collegiate Institute, in Toronto, for twenty-seven years and was the Head of the Modern Languages Department at that school for the last ten. He also served as Head of Modern Languages at Malvern Collegiate Institute for three years. Now retired, he devotes his spare time to being an active member of La Troupe des Anciens de l'Université de Toronto, traveling, gardening and writing for pleasure. *A Proud Azorean: A Biography* is the second volume of *An Azorean Trilogy*. Roberto is married and the boastful father of a wonderful daughter. He lives in Mississauga, Ontario, Canada.

www.ingramcontent.com/pod-product-compliance
Lightning Source LLC
Chambersburg PA
CBHW061745070526
44585CB00025B/2802